PACE'S
POST

PACE'S POST

Ramblings Of Wisdom
From A Middle-Aged Doc

VICTOR M. PACE, MD, FAAFP

Columbus, Ohio

PACE'S POST: Ramblings Of Wisdom From A Middle-Aged Doc

Published by Gatekeeper Press
2167 Stringtown Rd, Suite 109
Columbus, OH 43123-2989
www.GatekeeperPress.com

The cover design, interior formatting, typesetting, and editorial work for this book are entirely the product of the author.

Library of Congress Control Number: 2020947074

ISBN (paperback): 9781642375299
eISBN: 9781642375183

CONTENTS

DEDICATION

To my parents

INTRODUCTION

I never intended to write a book.

After I became a co-editor for a medical journal, I started writing monthly medical-related articles in a regular column titled *Pace's Post*. Discovering that writing was a relaxing diversion from my hectic and stressful life as a physician, I decided to write about topics that I felt were important to address. These topics ranged from subjects in which I have life experience to content that is fun and interesting.

The topics I have chosen cross all ages, genders, and orientations. In essence, they are pertinent to everyone. I would be remiss if I didn't put a disclaimer for the activities noted in the chapters. Skydiving or scuba diving, for example, are not reasonable activities for everyone; therefore, any participation is clearly at the discretion and risk of the reader.

While I take no responsibility for your actions, I do hope that you will live life to the fullest. I hope that you will get the most that you can out of your life, no matter what risk you are willing to take. Of course, any health issues, concerns, or medical clearances should be discussed with your medical team.

We get ahead in life with the assistance of others. Though we may have done the majority of the work, someone held the door open or steadied the ladder so that we could make our ascent and cross over into success. With that being said, I have so many people to thank in my life that I would have to write another book to mention them all. But I feel compelled to name a few ....

Thank you, Dr. David Muegge, for pulling me into the editorial community and engaging me in the writing world.

Thank you, Dr. Jim Blaine and Cathy Leiboult, for keeping me engaged in the writing process and for being my friends.

Thanks to my wonderful in-laws, Tony and Carol Strickland, for being amazing parents to my wife and for taking the time and energy to review my chapters as I wrote them.

Thanks to my daughter, Ling Pace, for doing her best and for caring for this world. You are a beautiful soul.

Thanks to my wife, Angie Pace, for being patient with me, supporting me, and simply loving me.

Thanks to all my other family members and friends, especially my twin brother Vincent Pace for being my friend growing up. And thanks to my parents Norma and Bob Pace. You both (Dad, I know you can hear me from heaven above) have shown your sons unconditional love and gave me a strong foundation where I was able to catapult from and be a positive influence in this world.

OK, that is enough thanking for now. Let's go ahead and dive into the depths of this book. This book is not meant to be a quick read—one you skim through and forget about. This book will help you see the world in a different light, with a perspective that you might not have thought of before. Or it might simply be a means to reinforce your current beliefs. In any case, I hope and pray that every one of you will get the most out of life and leave the world in a better place than you found it.

Risk-Taking

We all take risks in our daily lives.

Some risks give us 99 percent assurance that our outcome will be as expected. We trust that our pasteurized milk will not make us ill, that the car at the intersection will stop at the red light as we drive through, and that our alarm clock will go off at the exact time we had set it for. Some of us take on more risks by purchasing a home, getting involved in the stock market, or even getting married. These risks can be mitigated, however, by careful planning and preparation.

Having participated in all of those activities and also engaging in much higher-risk behaviors, I can attest that risk is both frightening and exhilarating. I improved my odds by becoming more knowledgeable. I practiced and educated myself on the benefits and risks of each activity. While these activities brought me much joy, they also left me with memories that will last a lifetime.

The first risk I took, I took with my hard-earned money. I come from a family that enjoys the game of chance, and my family frequented Las Vegas, Nevada, quite a lot in my childhood. It was no surprise that as an adult, I took an interest in casino gambling. I must preface this story with the fact that I never gambled more than I could lose and that I went into the activity with the realization that I was likely going to lose my initial bankroll. I have optimized my odds against the casinos by learning how to count cards.

Back in the 1990s, if you wanted to gamble in my hometown, you had to be on the water. If my cousin and I wanted to gamble, we would trek on over to the *Alton Belle*. The *Alton Belle* was a small riverboat casino that would take gaming excursions up and down the Mississippi River. On one of our outings, I lost $195 out of my $200 bankroll within the first fifteen minutes of the ride. We had a two-hour ride ahead of us, so it looked like I would simply be watching my cousin gamble; this is not a gambler's idea of fun. But the cards ultimately turned in my favor and my last five-dollar bet snowballed into $885. That night was an epic roller coaster ride that I have never been able to replicate.

Speaking of roller coasters, I used to love visiting amusement parks and going on all the scary, turbulent, and unpredictable rides. These days, due to the aging process, I limit my rides to the carousel, and even that can induce a vertiginous reaction. Yet, carousel rides do not leave the same impression on me that the scream-inducing rides did.

One memorable ride I went on was when my wife and I visited Silver Dollar City in Branson, Missouri. The park was open past dark. While riding roller coasters in the daytime seemed to satisfy us, riding them backward in the dark took the rides to an entirely different level.

Years ago, I visited Disney's Hollywood Studios. I opted to take a ride on the Tower of Terror. At that time, I didn't know much about the ride. I found the inline wait time to be engaging, since there was a *Twilight Zone* theme. Once I was buckled into the elevator-like lift, I found myself feeling quite frightful. I was unknowingly, unwittingly, and gradually taken to the top of the ride, several stories in the air. The doors in front of us opened up and we all found ourselves high above ground, staring at the park in front of us. You could feel the awe, the wow factor, that my fellow riders and I were experiencing. Then suddenly, and without warning, we were on a free fall back to the ground.

I have always loved the free fall sensation associated with wild and crazy amusement park rides. So, after I graduated from college, I decided to do a true free fall. My brother and I, along with several of our friends, decided to go skydiving. We set a date, and as the days passed, our friends dropped out one by one until only my brother and I remained. The day came, and we needed to get up in the wee hours of the morning to drive to the drop zone. I could not persuade my brother to get up, so I ventured out on the adventure, scared and alone. I left my parents a note letting them know where I was, just in case they had to scrape me up from the ground.

After spending all morning practicing as well as getting instructed on the skydiving basics, our group was finally ready to do a real, live jump. At the time, in order to be eligible for a free fall, you had to complete five successful static line jumps. A static line jump is where your ripcord is attached to the plane, and your parachute bag automatically opens up when you jump out of the plane. I quickly knocked out the five static line jumps, and I was eligible for the free fall jump. Interestingly, I was not nervous at all with the static line jumps, but the thought of doing a free fall jump was terrifying to me. I wasn't doing a tandem jump with the instructor; I was doing a free fall all by myself.

The skydiving plane we were in was small. The three of us neophytes, plus our instructor, were compacted into the hollow shell interior like sardines. We were all on our knees, and when it was your turn, you would need to protect your equipment and scoot to the opening. If the person in front opted not to jump, then none of the others sitting behind them could jump out of the plane; the plane would need to land and let that person deplane that way. Unfortunately for me, the first guy in our free fall group opted not to engage in his first free fall, so it looked like we had to land the plane. When you are in the process of skydiving, you don't want to get to the ground with a plane landing. Next thing I know, the instructor coerced the guy to put his feet out onto the platform above the wheel, and suddenly the guy was no longer in the plane. My mind was racing as I imagined that the instructor pushed the guy out. Suddenly, I was petrified.

It was now my turn to perform my first free fall skydive. The plane was at an altitude of about 3,500 feet, high enough to understand that death was possible and low enough to see what impact would do to the body. I scooted up towards the plane's opening and positioned myself. I was ready to disembark one last time. I held onto the plane's interior as I carefully lifted my feet up and over the edge, placing them onto the exterior platform. I grabbed the bracing underneath the wing and inched my way towards the strut of the wing. I was dangling off the exterior of the plane; I was to let go and fall backwards once we reached the jump site. I waited for my instructor to give me the signal, and once he did, I let go, counted to three, and then pulled the rip cord. The canopy extracted from my parachute bag, and I felt the sensation that I was catapulted upward. Instantly, I found myself gliding downward as I toggled myself to the drop zone target and then landed safely on the ground. To this day, I still have my free fall certificate and the photo of my head hanging out of the plane.

Opting to leave skydiving to the experts, I chose to try something closer to the ground. After taking lessons and purchasing my own equipment, I spent the next few years rock climbing; it is a great hobby as well as good exercise. Back when I first took up this sport, there were no commercial rock climbing walls in my area. In order to rock climb, you had to go and find a rock to climb. I mainly engaged in top-rope climbing, a style in which a rope and anchor system are utilized, with a belayer, or a climbing partner. It is important to have a second person there to protect the climber, as well as to take up slack from the rope so the climber only has to fall for a short distance. This is crucial should the climber lose their grip and spiral to the ground.

I thoroughly enjoyed rock climbing, and I continued to climb through the end of my medical school years. I recall one memorable day when I was top climbing up a cliff in Missouri. I reached the cliff's apex and was just about to celebrate when I was taken by surprise. A few hikers were above me at the cliff's edge. The lady yelled out for me to look up. As I did, she took a snapshot of me. The camera's flash startled me, and I let go of the cliff. Suddenly, I was reliving my skydiving days all over again. Fortunately, my belayer was paying attention, and I only dropped about twenty feet.

Over time, I gave up reaching for the sky and decided to head below the ground.

And no, I don't mean hell.

After several months of training and preparation, I finally received my Professional Association of Diving Instructors

(PADI) divemaster certification. Scuba diving took me to exotic areas as well as local rivers and lakes. I was able to dive in an old lead mine in Bonne Terre, Missouri. I saw that the rocks really were shaped like tables at Table Rock Lake. I chartered and helped sail a diving sailboat to the Bahamas, and I almost drifted away off the coast of Mexico.

Though I have had several memorable dives, four dives in particular stick out in my mind. My dive partner and I were diving in the Bahamas at a depth of about thirty feet. There was a slight current present, and we were bracing ourselves on the sandy sea floor. After checking my surroundings, I quickly realized that I wasn't holding onto the sand, but I was supporting myself on the dorsal fin of a small nurse shark. I let go, and fortunately for me, the shark decided to leave me alone and not swim away with my hand. Excited and wanting to share this moment with my dive partner, I motioned to him at the same time he was motioning for me to look up. We were in awe, as we saw about ten nurse sharks swimming above our heads. They quickly dissipated, and we headed back to the boat to tell our tale.

The next dive took place on the coast of Panama City, Florida. I had just finished a dive and was waiting on the surface to get back onto the dive boat. While I was waiting, without warning, a bottlenose dolphin poked its head above the surface of the water. We were now facing one another. We gazed into each other's eyes for what seemed like an eternity, and then the dolphin swam away.

I was back in the Bahamas and I was doing my first night dive. The moon was full and brightened the first few feet of the ocean water. After descending to about twenty feet with our lights off, I found myself in a pitch-black environment. It was so dark, I couldn't even see my hand when it was placed in front of my face. I turned my light back on only to see one of the diver's legs was swaying back and forth next to a coral reef. A large eel kept sliding in and out of the coral's opening, and it appeared that this eel was fixated on the diver's leg. I did let the diver know, but devilishly, I really did want to see what the eel was going to do.

Before any official training and before my divemaster days, I took my very first dive off the north shore of Oahu, Hawaii, at Shark's Cove. I was accompanied by a dive instructor and divemaster. We descended next to the coral reef, when the dive instructor spotted a small squid. He apparently wanted to have this discovery for lunch, so he pulled out his dive knife and started to stab the squid with the blunt end of his knife. The squid outsmarted him, though, and grabbed onto the knife handle. It then started jabbing the sharp end of the knife at the diver. The diver bounced around to avoid a stabbing, and then the squid squirted out some ink, dropped the knife, and zipped away, leaving the diver without his lunch.

They say that the greater the risk, the greater the reward. Perhaps this is true, but it is up to us to determine what risks we are willing to take in our lives. The key is to figure that out and then go for it with all of our gusto. I am glad I've taken the risks I have in my life, and I have few, if any, regrets.

A Day in the Park

Have you ever sat on a park bench and wondered about the lives of the people around you?

One spring day, I was sitting on a park bench and envisioning the thoughts of the four people around me. There was an elderly man, a young mother with two children, a college-aged female, and a middle-aged man.

Thinking about this moment from their perspectives, this is what I saw that day. I was taking a break from a long day at work and I just wanted to unwind. It was a typical spring day, with temperatures in the low seventies and a slight breeze blowing in the air. Squirrels were frolicking in the grass, foraging for food, and looking for places to hide and bury their treasures. The sun's rays were peeking through the leaves on the trees, emitting a nice warmth over my face. The warmth from the sun's rays was just enough to balance the coolness from the breeze.

I thought about what I had accomplished for the day. I questioned if I helped my patients make the correct medical decisions for themselves. I started to think about the days and weeks ahead, only to remind myself that I needed to stay in the moment.

I returned to the beauty of nature, the wonders that God had bestowed upon me and for me. A rabbit was nibbling on some grass as its wide eyes glistened from the sun's reflection. I could hear the whooshing sound of the breeze as it blew by my ears. The wind also carried the gentle, flowery scent of the citrus sorbet daffodils blooming upwind. The daffodils speckled the greenery around them with bright, vivid orange and yellow colors that were oh, so palatable to my eyes. In the distance, I saw two teenagers riding their bikes, while a couple of lovers walked by on the sidewalk in front of me. I could tell that they were enamored with one another as each of them gazed into the other's eyes, smiling and laughing as they passed by.

"What A Wonderful World," the song so beautifully sung by Louis Armstrong, came to mind, and I felt so blessed that I was living and experiencing the world at this moment. Out of the blue, I recalled watching a video titled *Empathy: The Human Connection to Patient Care* from the Cleveland Clinic. I was reminded of the significance and importance of empathy when I deliver medical care to my patients. That is also when I began to wonder about the people around me. These individuals were experiencing the exact same moment as I am; yet, their experiences were so different from mine.

The middle-aged man had come out to the park today to find inspiration. He was pondering the times when he could create a song in one sitting. The lyrics and music would easily flow from his brain to his mouth, to his hands, and lastly, to his pen as the ink dried onto the paper. But these days, his mind was stumped with writer's block, and he was trying hard to push through this obstacle. So he sat on the moist ground in the middle of the city park, looking for a spark to relight the flame of his gift to the world.

As he sat on the lush grass, his mind began to wander. His writer's block was still in full control, but this time he did not fight it. He started to think about a time when he sat on this same grassy field, in this same park, on a beautiful and similar spring day years ago. The memory became so vivid that he had the sensation he was reliving it once again. The old sounds, smells, and sights rushed into his mind, and he recalled the song he wrote that day. That song would change the course of his life and catapult him into a world of fame and fortune. But that song faded over time, as did his wealth and recognition. He didn't care about materialism, as his main goal was to have the world be touched by his music. He succeeded for a time, with that song. As he thought about that memory, a flame suddenly started to flicker. His brain was whirling with lyrics once again; this time new fresh lyrics were created. The block had become the catalyst to help his creative juices flow, and he was finally able to generate a new song. This song was so powerful, so uplifting, that it would one day instill hope into the mind and soul of a young girl contemplating suicide, thereby saving her life. After he finished composing his new song that he would soon unleash onto the world, he got up and walked home, satisfied with his time spent in the park.

As the musician headed home, he passed by a disheveled elderly man sitting on the corner of the park bench. The elderly man had just come across the street from the hospital where his wife has been admitted for a terminal illness. He had been told earlier this morning that she would succumb to her illness. He was waiting for his daughter to arrive, and in the evening, they would transfer his wife back home. Hospice had been consulted, and the family had decided that his wife, the mother of his children, would want to spend her final days in the familiar surroundings and comfort of her home, rather than the sterile environment of the hospital.

The elderly man's mind was racing as fast as it did when he was thirty years old, the age he married his wife. Fifty-seven years had passed since the day of his marital bond, fifty-seven glorious years. He recalled the day they walked down the church aisle, a day not much different from that day. The sun was shining, the birds were chirping, and love was in the air. Like looking through a photo album, seconds slipped by as he reminisced on each snapshot—the precious moments he had shared with the love of his life. The bad times were forgotten and only the good times remained in his mind. His three beautiful children would be with him later in the evening when they gathered together to say goodbye to his spouse, their mother.

As he sat there on the bench, at the edge of the park, he began to weep. His emotions were entangled as he thanked God for a lifetime of joy and happiness. He thanked God for giving him and his family the strength and the courage to get through the difficult times in their lives. He thanked God for uniting him with his wife and for their sharing of so many memories for so many years. But he was also frightened as he sat there on the bench, at the edge of the park, on that spring day.

How would he survive without her? He did not want to wake up in the morning to an empty home. As he contemplated his feelings and thoughts, his daughter pulled up in her car. She had come to pick him up so they could take his wife, her mother, home one last time.

Just thirty feet from the elderly man, a young woman sat on a bench next to the play area. She had brought her two young children to the park that day so that they could play, like children all should. She lived in a high-rise apartment nearby with her husband and children. She liked to take her children to the park frequently so that they could see, feel, and touch nature, rather than staying in the confined apartment with its rooms high above the ground. She loved to hear the sweet sound of her children giggling and chattering in the distance as they romped through the playground.

She was absorbing the moments as they swung on the swings, slid down the slides, and played tag with one another. She understood that these moments would one day turn into memories, so she absorbed and relished her time with them now. For her, watching her children play was like the joy one had when coming face to face with a wild dolphin in the sea for the first time or when one tasted the succulent juices of a watermelon. She started to contemplate what the future would hold for her children. She knew in her heart that she and her husband were doing their best to provide a strong and healthy foundation for their children to build upon. Realizing this, she sat on that bench, content and filled with hope and love.

On that same bench sat a young college-aged woman. This woman was in the middle of studying for her college spring semester finals. She was taking a much-needed break from her school's library, the building that overlooked the park. She had been in the library until closing for the past two weeks in order to cram for her exams. As a political science major, she was eager to start her summer internship at the state capitol in a few weeks. But she first needed to get over the hump of three more final exams.

She was not worried about the exams, as she felt she had prepared well enough in order to conquer them. She did, however, contemplate her future. Would she have a successful career? Would she get married? Would she sit on a park bench in the future with children of her own, like the lady she was sitting next to today? She wondered if she could have it all. She wondered what sacrifices she would have to make in order to reach her goals. She tried hard to stay in the moment, but as hard as she tried, she was always thinking about something else. Even when she was here, she was always thinking about "there," so to speak. She wondered if that would ever change. She wondered how to make it change. As the moments passed, she realized her time was up, and she headed back to the library.

I began to wonder about our world and the people in it. Wouldn't our lives be better if we wondered more about others by putting ourselves in their shoes? The next time you get agitated at the driver who is driving slowly in front of you, you could wonder if maybe it is because their passenger was just released from the hospital after a major surgery and the driver is being extra cautious taking them home. The next time a stranger seems to be so abrupt, you could wonder if maybe it is because he or she just lost a job and is fearful about their future.

I do believe that when we have to take a stance on something or someone, we need to make sure it is worth the battle and worthy of our time. If we decide that it is, then we should charge forward with all our gusto and fortitude. However, if we can bend a little, with tolerance and love, in order to make this world a better place, then the correct choice becomes obvious.

So the next time you are sitting on a bench, watching people come and go, put yourself in their shoes for just a minute. Try to understand and appreciate their perspectives. If you can, then you are thereby making this place a "wonderful world."

TECHNOLOGY THEN AND NOW

I have embraced technology. I love getting all the new gadgets when they hit the market. I have an iPhone, Apple Watch, iPad, Apple Pencil, and MacBook Pro. I look forward to the release of the new operating systems. Yet, at the same time, I miss the old days—days when cell phones, remote controls, and even the internet didn't exist for the general public. Why would I miss this lack of technology? That's like someone saying he prefers an outhouse over an indoor toilet. However, forty years from now, people will look at today's technology and think it was ancient. So, let's take a step back in time and see how technology has evolved, then and now.

SHOPPING THEN

Remember the times when we actually drove to the mall? We would go to a mall and spend hours perusing the merchandise. During Christmastime, my family and I would head downtown to the Famous Barr, just to window-shop, like in the movie, *A Christmas Story*.

The windows on the ground floor would be decorated and lit up with all of the newest clothing, electronics, furniture, and games. The line would wind around the building as my family and I eagerly awaited the night's unveiling on a frigid December evening. We oohed and aahed at all of the newest advances. After viewing the ornately designed and well-thought-out window displays, we would leave our window shopping behind and march into the building for some actual shopping. Of course, the highlight for me and my brother was on the top floor. It was where we would wait to see Santa Claus, at Winter Wonderland.

As a child, I was an avid comic book reader. One of the most exciting parts of the comic book was the merchandise ad page. I would save up my allowance for several weeks in order to purchase items such as X-ray glasses, Sea Monkey pets, and a seven-foot nuclear submarine. All transactions were done through the mail. I would impatiently wait for eight to twelve weeks for my item to arrive. By the tenth week, I would run to the mailbox every day to see if my treasure was there; the anticipation was exhilarating. Sometimes the item would be a disappointment, but more often than not, the final product was worth the wait.

SHOPPING NOW

Today, when I want to go shopping, I rev up my computer or I pull out my smartphone. I would either surf the web or I would open up an app. I hardly ever go to the physical store anymore. If I need an office supply, home knick-knack, or novelty item, I pull up the store's website, order the item, and wait for the item to get delivered; the item is usually delivered within forty-eight hours. I enjoy picking out gifts on the internet, as I can find unusual items I never would have discovered at a big-box store. We even get our groceries delivered to us. My wife picks out the items online and they get delivered to our doorstep. I still head over to our favorite restaurants to pick up dinner, but only after I have already ordered the food online. I then pick it up curbside and come home and serve dinner to my family. These days, I can even have my smartphone scan my body and have custom-designed clothes delivered to my home. In the future, when electric automobiles become the norm, I won't even have to go to the gas station anymore.

COMMUNICATION THEN

When I was a child, we had a rotary-dial telephone attached to the wall. In order to enter in the seven-digit code (dial a number), you would have to rotate a numbered dial with your finger placed in the corresponding number's hole on the telephone's face. You would first pick up the phone's receiver that was attached to the telephone unit via a cord and make sure there was a dial tone. It was such a tedious ordeal that we were so excited when the rotary dial was replaced by a numeric keypad. I also remember going to my grandmother's home, picking up her rotary-dial telephone, and being mesmerized by what I heard on the other line. My grandmother actually shared her telephone line with other users.

When I first was on call, I was given a pager. When the pager went off, I would have to call the on-call service to retrieve my message. I would have to treat every page as an emergency because I wouldn't know how important the message was until I called the service. One disheartening time was when I was at the movies watching *Alien Resurrection* when my pager went off fifteen minutes before the ending. I returned to the movie only to see the credits rolling on the screen. So, I was really excited when my pager was upgraded to one that transmitted messages. Since I didn't have a cell phone back then, I would have to find a pay telephone and then make sure I had enough change in order to pay for the call.

When I received my first cell phone, it was a large bag phone with an equally large charger. The unit was about the size of a small backpack. At the time, I was truly concerned that I might get cancer from this monstrosity. Fortunately, advances were made, and my follow-up cell phones were able to fit in one hand.

COMMUNICATION NOW

When the iPhone came out in 2007, I said that only the gadget gurus would want one, as I was satisfied with my flip phone. By 2009, I purchased my first iPhone, an iPhone 3. Now, I sport an iPhone 11 Pro, and I couldn't be happier—that is, until the next iPhone comes out. I don't have to search the streets for a pay phone anymore. I don't need a pager anymore. I can look up practically any number on my phone. I can choose to send text messages, emails, faxes, have video chats, and yes, even make actual phone calls directly from my smartphone. Never say never, but I hope to never, ever have to use a non-smartphone again.

DIRECTIONS THEN

In 1975, my family was heading to Florida for a family vacation. I remember my parents having their United States Atlas sprawled out on the kitchen table. My dad would meticulously measure the different routes in order to find the shortest and fastest route to our destination. When they upgraded to a AAA (American Automobile Association) membership, we were excited to have the work done for us with TripTiks, a completely optimized mapped road trip from starting point to destination.

As a teenage driver, I always had a local map in my glove compartment. I would often have to pull over on the road, take out the map, and figure out either where I was or where I was going. Other times, I would ask an individual how to get somewhere. There were even times when I couldn't find my destination and was just happy to be able to find my way back home.

DIRECTIONS NOW

These days, I have a map in my glove compartment, for use only in case of an apocalypse. I have not pulled it out in years, and I hope that I never have to use one again. I did, however, teach my daughter how to read a paper map just in case of Armageddon. In place of my foldable map that has been collecting dust, I now have a smartphone equipped with a GPS device and map apps. I can either type in my destination into the map app's search bar or ask Siri, my voice-controlled personal assistant, to map my destination. Within seconds, I get a detailed step-by-step, road-by-road route, along with alternate routes based on time and distance. My Apple Watch, being paired with my iPhone, taps me on my wrist when I need to make a turn. With the aid of my smartphone, I now feel safer driving around unfamiliar areas.

INFORMATION THEN

When I had a term paper to write back in high school and college, I would have to trek on over to the library in order to obtain the information needed to complete my research. I would peruse the card catalog, the library's physical catalog of its contents, or search for items on microfiche, a flat piece of film containing documents, in order to gather the material needed for my paper. After gathering my books of reference, I would spend hours reading through the books to find information that was pertinent to my term paper. Often, I would end up checking out as many reference books as I was able and would trudge them back to my dorm room to read later. Doing research back then was almost as physically taxing as it was mentally taxing.

My wife recalled a time in the late 1980s when she took a family trip to Monterey, California. She spent countless hours making phone calls and gathering information through the mail (no, not email) from chambers of commerce, hotels, airlines, and sites of interest. Travel agents back then were not easily accessible in her small Georgia hometown.

INFORMATION NOW

It used to take my wife weeks to collect data for her California trip, but now it takes only minutes. What used to take me multiple trips to the library now can be done in the convenience of my home. The availability of the internet to the general public has forever changed how we live our lives. Information gathering is now instantaneous and efficient.

Smartphones pushed the envelope further, as now the information is at our fingertips. I have 292 apps on my iPhone, which include over 10,000 pages of medical books, access to over one million songs, over 22,000 personal photographs, as well as my fitness and food journals since 2009. I can start writing on my computer and finish it on my iPhone. My handheld smartphone has as much power as many personal computers.

What is so fascinating and interesting about technology is that we believe we have the greatest and best thing until the next greatest and best thing becomes available. When I was a child, it would be years before the next best thing was available. Now, we are moving at warp speed. If you blink, then you just might miss it.

WHY EVERYONE SHOULD VISIT MY HOMETOWN

Many of us St. Louisians are so proud of our hometown that we can sometimes nauseate the people around us with our zealous love for everything St. Louis. Since I have a platform to extend this love, I am going to take advantage of it. Many visitors' guides have already been written on St. Louis. I recommend that you get a free copy of this year's *Official Visitors Guide St. Louis* by going to explorestlouis.com. You can either request a printed copy or, if you want a more environmentally friendly option, download the digital version.

So why write about St. Louis when a comprehensive guide already exists? The simple answer is because I'm from St. Louis, and that's what we do: promote our city to everyone, whenever we can. I am not going to attempt to recreate the guide listed above but rather give you my perspective on what I believe makes St. Louis the greatest city on Earth.

St. Louis History

- St. Louis was founded in 1764 as a fur-trading post by Pierre Laclede Liguest and his 13-year-old scout, Auguste Chouteau, with a land grant from the King of France.

- The migration to St. Louis started in 1803 after the Louisiana Purchase Expedition of Lewis and Clark.
- Between 1840 and 1860, many new immigrants, particularly Germans and Irish, arrived in St. Louis, followed by waves of Italians, Serbians, Lebanese, Syrians, and Greeks.
- The Old Courthouse in Downtown St. Louis held two landmark cases in American history: the Dred Scott Case in 1847 (African-American freedom) and the Virginia Minor Case in 1873, (women's right to vote); sadly, both suits were denied.
- The city was mainly under Union control during the American Civil War despite Missouri being a divided state.
- St. Louis was the nation's first home-rule city and, by the 1890s, the nation's fourth-largest city.
- One of our city's greatest moments occurred in 1904, when St. Louis hosted the World's Fair. That year, the city hosted the Louisiana Purchase Exposition (in Forest Park), the 1904 Olympic Games (at Washington University's Francis Field), and the 1904 Democratic National Convention (at St. Louis Exposition and Music Hall).
- Although St. Louis has a high Catholic population, every major religion is represented and available in our area.
- Revitalization of St. Louis took place with the opening of the iconic Gateway Arch on June 10, 1967. This 630-foot monument, standing tall near the edge of the Mississippi River, now defines our city.

Attractions

- First, explore the museum underneath the Gateway Arch. Next, take a tram to the top of the arch and get a bird's-eye view of downtown St. Louis. Then, take a few steps over to the Mississippi River to ride on an authentic paddle boat.
- Attend a sporting event with both the World Champion St. Louis Cardinals (baseball) and the Stanley Cup Champion St. Louis Blues (hockey). In 2022, you'll be able to see a Major League Soccer St. Louis team play in a designated soccer stadium. In the meantime, attend a St. Louis Ambush indoor soccer game, or any other of the many sports at our numerous colleges and universities.
- Spend an entire weekend in Forest Park. See animals playing at the St. Louis Zoo, travel to the stars at the St. Louis Science Center & Planetarium, go back in time at the Missouri Historical Society, be inspired at the St. Louis Art Museum, or catch a musical outdoors at the Muny.
- You can even walk the same area that fairgoers did in 1904 at the World's Fair Pavilion, paddle around Post-Dispatch Lake and then eat lunch at the Boathouse, play a round of golf at Norman K. Probstein Golf Course, ice skate outside Steinberg Rink, stop and smell the roses at the Jewel Box, or just simply absorb nature on 1,300 acres in the middle of an urban setting.
- Once one of the largest and busiest passenger rail terminals in the world, Union Station now houses a AAA Four Diamond Hilton hotel, the 120,000 square foot St. Louis Aquarium, the 200-

foot St. Louis (Ferris) Wheel, a carousel, mini golf, a mirror maze, a rope course, and several restaurants. At Christmastime, you can board the Polar Express Train to the North Pole.

- Families will enjoy exploring the City Museum, Citygarden, Grant's Farm, the Magic House, and Sophia M. Sachs Butterfly House. There are also thrilling rides at Six Flags St. Louis and fascinating tours of the Anheuser-Busch Brewery.
- Visit "79 acres of beautiful horticultural display" at the Missouri Botanical Garden (known by St. Louisians as Shaw's Garden), founded in 1859. This is the nation's oldest botanical garden in continuous operation.

The Arts Scene

- The Fabulous Fox Theatre, opened on January 31, 1929, with a capacity of 4,500. It now presents over 200 performances and special events annually.
- Jazz St. Louis is a nonprofit organization whose mission is to "advance the uniquely American art of jazz through live performances, education, and community engagement."
- The St. Louis Symphony Orchestra is in its 140th season, and it is also a Grammy Award-winning symphony.
- Chaifetz Arena, on the campus of St. Louis University, is a 10,600-seat venue that hosts over 150 events yearly.
- Stifel Theatre is a historic theater located downtown. It opened in 1934 and now hosts a wide variety of events.

- The Grandel is an intimate theater experience in the Grand Central Arts District.
- The Sheldon hosts over 350 events each year, including jazz, folk, and classical music in the Concert Hall. It also has a wide range of exhibits that are held at the art galleries.
- The Dome at America's Center, a multi-purpose indoor downtown stadium, is used for concerts, motocross and truck events, major conventions, trade shows, and exhibitions.

Dining

Thousands of restaurants exist in the St. Louis area, ranging from fast food to fine dining. The official guide lists a lot of them, but there are so many that are not listed. However, you can find them online, through mobile apps, and through local magazines/pamphlets. I'm just going to list a few of my favorites.

- Cunetto House Of Pasta (Hill area) — huge food portions, reasonable pricing, ornate setting.
- McGurk's (Soulard area) — Irish food, three bars with a stage, outdoor garden seating.
- 360 Rooftop (Downtown area) — rooftop bar, full food menu, bird's-eye view of Busch Stadium.
- St. Louis Ballpark Village (Downtown area) — adjacent to Busch Stadium, several food choices, bars, entertainment; a baseball fan's paradise.
- Tony's (Downtown area) — fine dining; expensive but worth it.
- Olympia Kebob House & Taverna (Richmond Heights area) — my favorite Greek restaurant.

Accommodations

I must preface this section by stating that I really never have stayed in a St. Louis hotel. However, my friends and family have, so I feel comfortable promoting the three listed below. I have physically walked the grounds of these hotels and I would eagerly stay at any one of them. For a comprehensive list, refer to the official guide referenced above.

- The Chase Park Plaza Royal Sonesta St. Louis — First opened in 1922, this is an elegant, opulent hotel sitting at the edge of Forest Park in the Central West End. It is centrally located and is also on the historic hotel list.
- Moonrise Hotel — A green boutique hotel located on the Delmar Loop with a rooftop bar.
- St. Louis Union Station Hotel — A AAA Four Diamond Hilton hotel located within Union Station.

Shopping

As with food and hotel options, St. Louis has abundant shopping options. I will list a few of my favorites.

- The Delmar Loop — Filled with specialty shops, clothing boutiques, and gift stores.
- Historic Cherokee Antique Row — Six blocks of antique, collectible, and specialty shops.
- St. Louis Premium Outlets — Just thirty minutes from downtown. It offers an outdoor mall-like setting with more than ninety designer name-brand outlet stores.
- Chesterfield Outlets — Offers very good prices and is located near St. Louis Premium Outlets.

Neighborhoods

St. Louis has many unique areas that are each worthy of a weekend visit. Below are a few highlights of each area. Keep in mind that there is so much more to these neighborhoods. You will be yearning for more time to visit each of them. In the past, these areas were so defined by socio-economic status that a standard St. Louis question used to be, "Which high school did you go to?"; in fact, there has even been a book written about it.

- Maryland Heights — Creve Coeur Park, WestPort Plaza.
- The Delmar Loop — Tivoli Theatre, Fitz's Bottling Company.
- The Ville — Sumner High School (the first African American high school west of the Mississippi).
- North County — St. Louis Lambert International Airport.
- Laclede's Landing — where St. Louis started, Big Muddy Blues Festival.
- Downtown — Gateway Arch, Union Station, Old Courthouse.
- Lafayette Square — Victorian homes, restaurants, and boutiques around a 150-year-old park.
- Soulard — oldest farmers' market west of the Mississippi, Mardi Gras celebration.
- Central West End — Forest Park, Washington University School of Medicine.
- Grand Center Arts District — Fabulous Fox, St. Louis Symphony Orchestra, St. Louis University.
- Cherokee Lemp Historic District — Cherokee Antique Row, Lemp Mansion.

- Maplewood — "somewhere between Mayberry and Metropolis is Maplewood."
- The Grove — dance clubs, music venues, restaurants, bars, and shops.
- South Grand — Tower Grove Park, Magic Chef Mansion.
- The Hill — Italian restaurants and traditional grocers, Piazza Imo.
- Carondelet — first public kindergarten in the nation, Carondelet Park.
- Kirkwood — Magic House, Amtrak Rail Station.
- Webster Groves — Webster University, Repertory Theatre of St. Louis.
- Clayton — Galleria, Washington University, Forest Park, vibrant downtown area.
- Chesterfield — Butterfly House, outlet malls, Top Golf.
- St. Charles — Historic Main Street, Christmas Traditions, Legends and Lanterns.

One tip that I wish to pass on is my discovery of the useful and handy ParkLouie (ParkMobile) App for my iPhone. This app allows me to secure and pay for parking at parking spots around St. Louis (and other cities). It even reminds me when my time is expiring, allowing me to add more time right from my phone.

So, that's my take on why you should come visit my hometown. It would take a lifetime to explore all that St. Louis has to offer, but even a short visit will whet your appetite enough to where you will yearn to experience more of this awesome city. My city, our people, will welcome you with open arms.

THE LOVE OF PETS

I cannot recall a time in my life when I was without a pet in my home. Growing up, one of my earliest and fondest memories was when my parents brought home two puppies for me and my brother. Certainly, as a result of dogs being introduced into my early developmental years, I have become keen on dogs—so much so, that some might even refer to me as a dog person. You all know that type of person, and while many people are attracted to dog people, there are others who despise us. My goal is not for you to become a dog person, however. It is for you to become open to the possibility of having some sort of pet in your life.

When I was in medical school, I really didn't have time to care for a dog or cat, so I chose to bring home a hamster. I had hamsters growing up, so I knew how to take care of them. I could even be gone for a few days and they would be just fine. So one day, I brought home Rocki, a female hamster that I named after Rocky Balboa, the fictional boxer in the movie *Rocky*. Rocki had a great life. She lived for over four years, which is longer than the typical lifespan of a hamster. She was given treats and lived in a plastic translucent tubular and modular system called a Habitrail, where she lived a luxurious life. When I would come home each evening, she would run up to the Habitrail's lookout tower, and I would pet her and present her with her daily treat. Rocki became my inspiration during the turbulent and arduous times of medical school.

After medical school, I packed my bags and headed to Savannah, Georgia, for my family medical residency program. For some odd reason, with Rocki now gone, I did not have the desire to have another pet hamster. Since I was a single male living in Georgia, I figured now was the time to think about having a bigger pet. So I ventured on over to the local Humane Society. I knew that I couldn't care for a dog, given that I would spend countless hours working in the hospital, so I thought about getting a cat. Whoa, I can sense the dog people scratching their heads, thinking I've gone to the dark side, since I was flipping over to being a cat person. Interestingly, many dog and cat people are as divided as the two main political parties in our country. However, by getting a cat, I could better understand those people who choose to have cats as pets. Unfortunately, I am allergic to cats, so picking one did seem pointless. I had exhausted my search that day at the Humane Society and I was about to leave the facility feeling alone and defeated. However, as fate would set in, the custodian came over to me and whispered in my ear.

He said, "You see that cat over there? She's been here for over five months. We are a kill shelter and we put down animals after they have been here for a certain amount of time. No one will put her down, as everyone loves her." I wondered why he was telling me this piece of information that was obviously supposed to remain a secret. He went on to say, "But I saw how that cat looked at you, and you two belong together." Next thing you know, Rocki—yeah, that's the name I gave her—was in my arms and I was signing the adoption papers. Needless to say, the staff there didn't seem to take a liking to me, as I was stealing their favorite pet.

Rocki saved my life. For those who are not aware, enduring a medical residency program is both exhausting and exhilarating, a roller-coaster ride of sorts. Back when I went through residency, we could work up to 120 hours per week. We were still in the process of learning, but we were expected to know things that we simply hadn't learned. One day we would be saving a life, whereas other days our mistakes would be costly. If I had to come home to an empty apartment after spending forty-eight hours on call, I might not have felt worthy to continue living with myself.

But every night when I came home, Rocki was on the edge of the couch, waiting to head-butt me with a hello, and, yes, I know, marking me. She purred so loudly as she greeted and loved on her human. Rocki went on to live twelve healthy years. She was a black cat with a white patch on her face and neck. Years of gazing out the window, with the sun shining down on her, eventually took its toll. Her life ended prematurely as she developed metastatic skin cancer from her sun exposure. Rocki showed me, and my wife, that cat people are special, too.

By 2004, my wife and I had relocated to Springfield, Missouri. We had been married for over six years, and we were starting to think about having a family. Like many couples, we thought we would have a trial run by first raising a pet dog. At that time, it was just a passing thought. But one fateful day, Maggie came into our lives. We would frequent the local Humane Society to get our regular dose of puppy love. On a sunny and warm November day back in 2004, we ventured into the Humane Society for yet another routine visit. We had just finished playing with the dogs, and as we were headed out, the facility personnel brought in two black puppies. My wife and I quickly picked one up, just to simply play with it for a few minutes. But in that moment, I knew our lives would change forever. My wife gazed into that eight-week-old puppy's eyes with a similar love and affection that she showed humans.

My wife's playtime with this little fur ball was coming to an end, and we had a decision to make; this decision was of utmost significance. We needed to either give the puppy to the next person in line and accept that someone else would adopt her, or never let her go. My wife never let that puppy go. We took Maggie to the pet store, letting her pick out some of her toys, and then headed home to unveil her forever home to her. My wife will tell you that Maggie was the best dog ever, and I would be hard pressed to disagree with her. Maggie showed us so much love. She was the best for cuddling, and she somehow knew just when and how much love to give to someone. Some will say that we are simply personifying a nonhuman creature, but if you knew Maggie, well, you just knew how special she was to us humans. Maggie is physically no longer with us, but she will forever remain in our hearts.

As my daughter Ling was growing up, she always wanted pets of her own. We started out with gerbils, but she was too young, and I was the one who ended up having to care for them. As she became old enough to demonstrate personal responsibilities, I decided it was time to get her some fish. Ling is responsible for feeding and taking care of her fish daily. I help clean the tank, but otherwise, she is in charge. This responsibility is important for the development of a child. Ling is now a teenager and I am so proud of her for showing love and care to her pet companions.

Along with the fish, we currently have three dogs in our home. Chip, our 45-pound black Lab mix male, Noelle, our 25-pound American Staffordshire Terrier mix female, and Abby, our 15-pound Miniature Pinscher mix female. All of our pets, with the exception of the rodents and fish, have been rescued. My wife and I believe that God's creatures are here to give us love, and it is up to us to protect and love them back.

If by now you are not convinced that a pet is right for you, think about these facts. The Centers for Disease Control and Prevention (CDC) states on their website the following information:

Studies have shown that the bond between people and their pets can increase fitness, lower stress, and bring happiness to their owners. Some of the health benefits of having a pet include the following:

- Decreased blood pressure
- Decreased cholesterol levels
- Decreased triglyceride levels
- Decreased feelings of loneliness
- Increased opportunities for exercise and outdoor activities
- Increased opportunities for socialization

So to the millions of pet owners in America and the world, thank you for creating that bond and protecting God's creatures. For those individuals and families that are contemplating bringing a pet into their home, do your homework and make sure that you connect with the right pet for you or your family. And for those who scorn or despise having a pet, you will eventually come around. It may happen when you are in the nursing home, bonding with the facility's pet birds, but you will come around; I have faith in you.

THE ADVENTURE OF
TREASURE HUNTING

Imagine finding yourself on a deserted island in the middle of the South Sea. You are wandering about the sandy shore. The waves from the sea are crashing at the break as the tide gently flows onto the beach. The leaves on top of the trees are flapping about as the wind whooshes in your ear.

Down below, you are cutting through the thick, dense foliage that has grown up over the years. As you meticulously venture into the unknown, you spot what you are looking for. The large boulder is where the X is marked on your map. As you start to vigorously dig with excitement and anticipation, you wonder if you have found it. Then, all of a sudden, your shovel is met with resistance and you hear a clunking sound as you attempt to dig farther. You start to go into hyperdrive, and as if you are living in a surreal world, you uncover an old wooden chest. Yanking the chest out of the ground, you knock off the rusty padlock and lift up the lid, and your wildest dreams come true. The coffer is filled with gold bullion coins, silver chalices, diamonds, and gems.

Back when I was growing up, searching for a hidden treasure was a dream of many children. One of our friends would hide an item for discovery in Francis Park or in a neighbor's yard and sketch out a rudimentary map of the area with an X marking the spot, and then the rest of us would head out on our adventure. I imagined myself being on an island similar to the one I had just described above, as my friends and I spent hours looking for our treasure.

Other days, our group of friends would hear of a rumor that a long-lost treasure was buried somewhere in our neighborhood. We would gather our tools, typically a flashlight and a compass, and head out for our day's adventure. The movies *Goonies* and *National Treasure* inspired the ultimate treasure hunts. These days, however, with "stranger danger" and the hazards of the world, children are typically not allowed to be unleashed alone, wandering about their neighborhoods without supervision.

However, there are still several ways in which one can participate in their own treasure hunt today. You can go to a yard sale or a flea market where your treasure is in full view, waiting for you to find it. By grabbing an inexpensive or more elaborate costly metal detector, you can scour a beach, back yard, or park to search for lost treasures. Some people opt to go dumpster diving, while others choose to recycle bottles and cans in exchange for a small profit.

One activity I loved so much as a child was to go down to the bank, purchase a few dollars in rolled pennies, and then go searching for that valuable penny. Often, I would discover a wheat or Indian head penny and my dream would come true for that day.

When I was a young man, I was invited by my friends to participate in an event called the Halloween Brewhaha. We were divided into teams of four, and the goal was to be the first team to arrive at a specified destination, where a prize would be given to the winners. As it was Halloween, we all were required to dress up, and my group chose to be vampires. I was dressed up as a police vampire. Our first clue, which we had to figure out, would lead us to a local bar in the downtown St. Louis area. From that clue, we would need to go to the bartender and give them the answer to the clue. Once that was accomplished, the bartender would hand over the next clue to us. We would then head out to the next location with the clue and repeat the process until all the participants converged at our final destination. That night was truly an adventure, and my team was declared the winner. I don't recall what the physical prize was, but the true prize was in the journey. Over thirty years have passed since that enchanting evening, and yet, I remember it as if it were yesterday.

If children are involved in your adventure, you wouldn't want to include bars and nightclubs, but you can certainly have a real, live adventure. Scavenger hunts are in vogue these days, and the preparation work has already been done for you. You can get your child excited about your next vacation by taking them on a journey around your newly discovered vacation spot. Equipped with your smartphone, your family, or just yourself, can see a city in a whole new perspective. You purchase the adventure from reputable companies and then head out to make memories.

Back in my Scouting days, we would pull out our paper maps and compasses, be given specific mapping coordinates of our goal location, and then meticulously and laboriously set out in search of our destination. This process could take hours as we would continuously have to remap our coordinates until we reached our goal. These days, anyone with the aid of their smartphone can participate in this adventure.

Geocaching is a game whereby players search for a cache using geographical coordinates with the aid of a GPS (Global Positioning System) device. Almost anyone can participate in this treasure hunt. You download the free app on your smartphone, search for caches in your area, and then head out to find your treasure, the cache. I wanted my daughter to have the same memory I had as a child with searching for a lost treasure. Geocaching has allowed us to share that experience together. Sometimes the cache is a nano-type container with only a log inside. Other times, the cache is a large box with multiple trinkets for trading.

Geocaching, previously termed geostashing, originated in the year 2000 in Oregon. That was when the first cache was hidden. According to geocaching.com, over three million caches are hidden throughout the world today. Back in August 2010, I discovered geocaching, and my daughter, wife, and I all set out on our adventure. We were vacationing in St. Petersburg Beach, Florida, at the time. Though we were unsuccessful in finding the hidden cache, we thoroughly enjoyed stumbling around unfamiliar territory.

Another fond memory of geocaching was one I shared with my in-laws. My family and I were again vacationing in Georgia, this time on St. Simons Island. We were on the island's main pier searching for our cache while being surrounded by muggles, otherwise known as people who were not involved in or unaware of geocaching. When muggles are around one's chosen cache, stealth moves become necessary. This is so the muggles will not discover what you are doing. I saw my mother-in-law return to her childhood as she helped us search for the cache. This time, we were not only successful in finding the cache, but in those moments, we created new memories for years to come.

Whatever treasure hunt you choose to engage in, there is an adventure suitable for nearly everyone. By your participation in one of these activities, you will find that your true discovery is in your journey.

MEDICALLY
THEMED MOVIES

I love going to the movies. When the dog days of summer beat down on us, there is nothing like sitting in a dark, air-conditioned movie theater. It is such a refreshing break from the steaming-hot weather outside. I believe that not only can we be entertained by a movie, but we can learn something from the movie as well. I have learned something from each of the medically themed movies noted below. I encourage you to see one or all of these movies if you have not already done so.

I was flying from Chicago several years back, before I was in the field of medicine, when I sat by a heavyset man. This man wanted to talk, and unfortunately, I was stuck in the middle seat, so I couldn't really get away from him. During our lengthy one-sided conversation, he informed me that he was involved in theater.

Finally, the lady sitting next to me, who happened to be a nurse, said loudly, "You don't know who he is, do you?"

Embarrassed, I just sat there dumbfounded while the man started getting tearful as he said, "Jack Nicholson made it big, Danny DeVito made it big, even Christopher Lloyd, but nobody knows me."

The nurse comforted him and spouted out his claim to fame. He then opened up his briefcase and gleefully began handing out autographed photos of himself alongside his theater buddies. And that's how I met Sydney Lassick, a.k.a. Cheswick from *One Flew Over the Cuckoo's Nest* (1975, R-rating). Having never seen this movie, I rented it when I returned home.

Considered a classic and one of the greatest films ever made, *One Flew Over the Cuckoo's Nest* is an American comedy-drama film. The main character, Randle McMurphy, played by Jack Nicholson, is a criminal who fakes being mentally ill in order to escape the drudgeries of prison life. He hopes to reside in an easy, relaxed environment but quickly learns that he has many challenges in the mental institution, especially with his nemesis, Nurse Ratched. I learned from this film that I did not want to be an inpatient psychiatrist, and it is best to befriend all the Nurse Ratcheds of the world.

As a physician, I give my patients daily marching orders that cause them to embark on a journey through the entanglements of medicine. For some, this is no more than a single laboratory test, but for others it can be an array of seemingly endless tests and appointments. The art of medicine reminds us to be empathetic and show compassion for our patients' individual journeys.

In the movie *The Doctor* (1991, R-rating), the main character, played by William Hurt, is a successful, wealthy, self-centered surgeon. He becomes inflicted with throat cancer and is thrust into the perils of being a patient himself. For really the first time, he sees the world from the patient's perspective, and it enlightens him to become a better human being. I was reminded by this movie to avoid the God complex that so many physicians have had before me, and I try to really put my feet in the patient's shoes.

Like many medical students, gross anatomy class was the bane of my existence during my first year of medical school. My gross anatomy lab partner was this brilliant, budding surgeon prodigy. He would examine our corpse and point out every single artery, vein, ligament, and tendon in the dissected area. I, on the other hand, would look at the same human cadaver and see a formaldehyde-pungent clump of internal organs that never seemed to match up to my well-organized *Netter's Atlas*.

Having seen the movie *Gross Anatomy* (1989, PG13-rating) prior to starting medical school, I was particularly nervous about taking the course, as it was viewed by many as the most difficult course in medical school. The movie focuses on a first-year medical student, played by Matthew Modine, and his interactions with his fellow classmates and instructors while enrolled in the gross anatomy class. His approach to medical school and life in general is challenged by the demands placed on him during this time. Yet, he is able to overcome this difficult time while maintaining his nonconformist view on life. This movie taught me to conquer the obstacle by focusing on the end goal, as well as sticking to the grind while maintaining my perspective on life.

As highly trained medical professionals, most physicians have the knowledge and expertise to address complicated medical issues. But sometimes, it is our own experiences that make all the difference to our patients. I recall a scene in *Doc Hollywood* (1991, PG13-rating) where such a response is so evident. The movie, starring Michael J. Fox, is about a young hotshot surgeon who is headed to Beverly Hills when he suddenly gets into an automobile crash. He is sentenced to community service at the hospital in Grady, South Carolina, where he encounters a 6-year-old cyanotic boy. He then diagnoses him with mitral valve regurgitation and informs the boy's parents that immediate surgery may be needed for a cardiac crisis. The town's curmudgeonly doctor intercepts them and recognizes that the child's cyanosis is from an overdose of bismuth subnitrate as a result of the child having chewed his father's tobacco. The boy is given a Coca-Cola to counter the bismuth and relieve the child's stomachache.

Several years back, my wife was in the hospital with a pulmonary embolism. While in the hospital, she developed a debilitating headache. The medical staff was about to give her an antiemetic and schedule her for a brain imaging study when I intervened. I realized that she had been in the hospital for two days without getting her usual dose of caffeine. So, like the old town doctor, I said, "Wait—hold on, and give her a Coke." Within fifteen minutes of her sipping the soda, her headache subsided and costly measures were averted. I don't know if my response to my wife's dilemma was based on my years of experience as a physician or simply remembering that scene in *Doc Hollywood*. What I do know is that the movie is a nice reminder about not overlooking the simple solutions.

By the time *Patch Adams* (1998, PG13-rating) arrived on the big screen, I was well into my third year of residency and struggling to smile during the day. Medical residency has a way of sucking the joy out of life. Medical residents must push through the daily and often difficult obstacles while trying to maintain their humanity. Patch Adams, played ironically by the late Robin Williams, is based on a true story of a suicidal medical student. Patch intertwines humor in his approach to his medical care, treating the spirit as well as the body of his patients. The timing of the movie's debut was significant for me as the movie reminded me that humor does not have to be avoided when dealing with patients. Bonding with my patients not only humanizes them but can also improve their medical outcomes.

One last film I would like to comment on is *M*A*S*H* (1970, R-rating). I have never been in the military, but now in my medical career, I am fortunate to be able to treat some of our nation's veterans. I will never have direct experience or knowledge of what these brave men and women have gone through during their military service, but I am able to have some understanding of their particular situations in indirect ways.

By going to the movies, I am given some insight into the horrors of combat and war. I want to reiterate that I will never have the same understanding or share the brotherhood/sisterhood that veterans have with one another by simply watching a movie. While several movies have been made about the military, *M*A*S*H* is a dark, dramatic comedy on many aspects of war. The movie follows the medical personnel unit of the 4077th Mobile Army Surgical Hospital stationed in South Korea in 1951. Two of the main characters, played by Donald Sutherland and Elliott Gould, show disdain for their unfortunate predicaments. They use horseplay and humor to maintain their sanity and yet still manage to rise to the occasion as excellent combat surgeons.

I have taken you through a quick tour of some of my favorite medically based movies that have had an impact on my life. I could spend hours listing several other movies that have had an influence on me, but I will defer that to another time. In the meantime, I hope to see you at the movies.

MY JOURNEY THROUGH RACISM

I have been advised not to write on the topic of racism because a privileged White male physician writing about racism would open up a can of worms, and it also might not sit well with the reader. But silence is on the side of racism, and I believe America needs to hear the perspective from my vantage point. The definition of racism is a belief that specific races produce inherent superiorities over other races simply based on one's race. So, are you a racist? I, unfortunately, discovered in my youth that I had racist views. Through the years, I have become more knowledgeable and wiser on these hateful beliefs, and I have worked to push out my racist thoughts. I will talk more on that later.

According to www.history.com, here are some historical facts on slavery in America:

- 1619 — *The White Lion* brings twenty African slaves to Jamestown, Virginia; this event is seen as the starting point to slavery in America.
- September 22, 1862 — President Lincoln issued a preliminary Emancipation Proclamation.

- January 1, 1863 — The Emancipation Proclamation becomes official and holds that "slaves within any State, or designated part of a State ... in rebellion, ... shall be then, thenceforward, and forever free."
- June 19, 1865 — Federal troops arrive in Galveston, Texas, taking control of the state and ensuring that all enslaved people are freed. Juneteenth celebrates this date and is considered the longest-running African American holiday.

Growing up in South St. Louis City, I was influenced by my environment. St. Louis was, and for the most part still is today, divided in communities based on ethnicity and race. Segregation was the norm. When a Black man walked into our neighborhood, I would see him get escorted out. I came to believe that a Black man was in our neighborhood only to create mayhem and trouble. I would hear conversations that the White male didn't get a certain job because the competition was a minority. I would hear the N-word used in casual conversation. My parents condemned racism, but they too were influenced by what they saw in their youth. My father had an auto parts store in a predominantly Black neighborhood. I would interact with the African American people in the homes across the street on Vandeventer Avenue, but some of them were crack dealers. So I came to believe that crack dealers were Black. The influences of nature and nurture affect a child's perspective, but still, this is no excuse for racism.

Other than being told that the above views are distorted, warped, and inherently wrong, how else can one stamp out racism and hatred, which are often synonymous terms?

The old adage "Before you judge a man, walk a mile in his shoes" is the key in understanding one's viewpoint.

When I was attending college in San Antonio, Texas, I wanted to pursue my boxing career that I had successfully started in high school. So one day, I ventured into a youth center on the west side of town, an area of San Antonio known for its toughness. As I walked into the boxing gym, I heard the word "gringo" and quickly realized that I was the only White person in the room. Spanish was the only language spoken in the gym, and the coach directed me with grunts and head nods. I was purposely mismatched with my sparring partner. Weighing in at 175 pounds, I was put in the ring with a boxer who weighed easily over 250 pounds. On top of that, he was wearing the speed bag gloves, ones you can feel the knuckles through. I, on the other hand, had the 18-ounce sparring bag gloves, ones that feel like getting hit with a pillow. Needless to say, I was pummeled. My nose was busted, I spit up blood for three days, and I was dizzy for a week. I was sent a clear message that I did not belong there simply because of the color of my skin. That day ended my aspiring boxing career, and I left dejected, feeling violated, angry, and frightened. However, I came out of that experience a better man, as it shattered the previous racist thoughts that I had growing up.

Now, envision a Black person living their life in America. I experienced the fear of being a minority for a few minutes, in a country where a person of color, particularly Black young males, has to endure this fear their entire existence. Whereas White parents will instruct their children on stranger danger, Black parents have to teach their children how to be submissive in order to stay alive.

Juneteenth is undoubtedly a progressive move in the history of our country. But it also put the Black person at a big disadvantage. Freed slaves were suddenly thrust into American culture, many without money, education, or the resources to better their lives. In many areas, they were still looked upon as inferior. Today, we still see racial inequalities in the treatment, health, and well-being of people of color. Yet, 155 years since Juneteenth, Black people have shown the world that they can overcome adversity and obstacles by becoming successful in areas of law, medicine, and education, to name a few. Now, there are people that will say they became successful because they were given advantages and that they played the race card. Who are they trying to fool? When a horse starts the race ten lengths behind its competitors and still wins the race, that is an impressive and deserving win. Even in a dead heat, the disadvantaged horse clearly won the race.

I will be the first to admit that, until the death of George Floyd, I didn't fully appreciate the sacrifice Colin Kaepernick made when he knelt during the National Anthem. His statement was never about disrespecting our flag. It was simply meant to bring awareness to the racial inequalities in our society. I have to admit that if I were a Black male, I would be a bitter man. I would have a chip on my shoulder knowing that my ancestors were shackled, beaten, and treated like savage animals. Yet, men and women of color have served in our armed forces and defended our country and our flag. I would be bitter in a country that celebrates Italian and Irish heritages but looks upon African folklore as if it were voodoo. Our brothers and sisters of color are hemorrhaging, especially the Black community, and we all must come together to stop the bleeding.

It is easy to point out racism but much harder to stamp out civil rights inequalities. Dr. Martin Luther King, Jr., envisioned a world where all men and women were treated equally and without bias. Laws will be enacted, reforms will be made, protests will occur, monuments will come down, but nothing will change until we instill true love into our society. Every major religion has love at the core of its faith. The Christian Bible (NIV version) best sums it up with 1 Corinthians 13:4-8:

> Love is patient, love is kind.
> It does not envy,
> it does not boast,
> it is not proud.
> It does not dishonor others,
> it is not self-seeking,
> it is not easily angered,
> it keeps no record of wrongs.
> Love does not delight in evil
> but rejoices with the truth.
> It always protects,
> always trusts, always hopes,
> always perseveres.
> Love never fails.

If we are to show the world that America is as great as we think it is, then we need to see Dr. King's dream through to the end.

THE VALUE OF
JOURNALING

When I was a child, it was typical for a young girl to keep a diary. Girls would write their most intimate thoughts on the pages. This was quite risky for them, since their deepest, darkest secrets and thoughts might get exposed by those with a wandering eye. The girl would typically hide her diary under her mattress or in her closet. As an added protection, diaries back then came with a lock and key, so only the key holder could access the book.

Boys, especially brothers, were notorious for trying to access a girl's thoughts. Concerned parents might even try to infiltrate the pages after a failed attempt to interrogate their child on a specific child-rearing matter. Although we lived in the same world then as we do now, the environments in this regard were far from discernible.

Keep in mind that young girls were not the only ones to keep journals at that time. Scientists kept journals to organize and report their scientific findings, discoveries, successes, and failures. Writers kept journals out of a creative necessity. Adults kept journals to gather their thoughts and to improve their mental psyche. The most famous of journals was arguably written by a Dutch-German child, who suffered the atrocities of an evil Nazi regime.

I have kept some form of a journal since 1983, and my journaling has evolved over the years. My first journal started out as a simple appointment book. I would write down everything I did for the day. As time passed and technology advanced, I began to keep a detailed appointment book of my day's events, many entries with notations, on an app on my smartphone. I suspect many of you are thinking, "What a waste of time! I've got better things to do."

Perhaps, but with the aid of my app, it takes me only a few minutes a day to capture and immortalize that day's events. I print out the entries each month and every so often, but always at the start of the New Year, I read through the printed pages. A person's memory of an event will fade over time. Yet a familiar scent, sound, or photograph can spark one's mind, allowing that person to recall all the details of a time that has passed as if it were yesterday. By reading through my appointment entries, I am able to recall a previously forgotten day vividly and memorably.

Remember the old cliche "a picture is worth a thousand words"? Again, with the aid of technology, I have been able to keep another journal, a photo journal. Growing up, I would not have been able to practically initiate such a task. But these days, a click of a button is all it takes to capture the moment for all to be able to see. I have kept a photo journal since 1999 and I currently have over 37,000 photos on my computer. These photos are divided into 216 photo albums. For about an hour each month, I select key photos, place them in a book layout, and then have the book published at the end of the year, a book that will be placed on our bookshelf for all to see. Sometimes, I organize and publish vacation books as well. My daughter thoroughly loves sitting down and perusing these photo journals.

I also keep a standard type journal. I don't keep a daily written journal; rather, I place entries into my personal journal when I am moved to do so. During the COVID-19 pandemic, I found myself opening up and writing in my journal almost every day. This allowed me to defuse my emotions, capture my ideas into words, and once again, immortalize my thoughts onto paper.

Finally, every Sunday morning, I write entries into my gratitude journal. I have done this since April 2015, and I find it to be one of my most rewarding journals that I keep. Using a specific app on my smartphone, I sit down every Sunday morning, usually before going to church, and write down what things I am most grateful for in the previous week. I attach up to three photos to that week's entry. At the end of the year, I print them all out and place them in a binder. I reread them periodically, but the true benefit of the journal is the simple acknowledgement of gratitude for the various things in my life. This task allows me to appreciate both my good and bad days, my ups and my downs—essentially every aspect of my existence.

By now, one might be thinking that I am obsessed with journaling and with these next few words, you might just be right. One final journal that I keep is a health journal. I keep a written record of all the exercise I have done, food I have eaten, and emotions that I am feeling for the day, as well as a weekly record of my weight. This makes me accountable for my health and well-being.

Even though I keep the multiple journals listed above, I am still able to keep my mind in the here and now, living life to the fullest, and living in the moment. My journaling does not cause me to be self-absorbed, but instead allows me to become more aware and appreciative of those around me. You may not desire to keep this many journals, but I believe that at least one type of journaling would be beneficial to all.

These days, some people opt to keep their journals public by blogging or vlogging on social media sites. For some, these means do not differ much from my journaling methods, except for the number of people having access to the journal. Though I choose not to open my life up to the microscopic, eternal nature of the internet, others find it both rewarding and exhilarating. I may certainly judge a specific journal entry viewpoint, but I would not judge their decision to make their journal open to the public.

To summarize the benefits of journaling, keeping a journal has the potential for the following effects:

- Reduces stress and anxiety and improves one's mood
- Boosts memory, concentration, and comprehension
- Instills happiness and enhances one's sense of well-being
- Allows for a better self-appreciation and gratitude
- Makes one accountable for their decisions
- Allows for a faster and healthier healing process
- Helps identify negative thoughts and fosters positive ones
- Sets and documents daily, extended, and life goals as they are achieved
- Improves one's writing and creative skills
- Slows down life and allows for self-reflection

The key to successful journaling is discovering which type of journaling is right for you and then just doing it.

BULLYING

When I was a child growing up in the inner city of St. Louis, Missouri, our respectable Catholic grade school class had a pair of bullies. These two hooligans would terrorize me and my classmates during recess and after school. They would get reprimanded at times, but the bullying persisted until we all graduated. It was a different time in America back then; the behavior of those individuals and others like them was seen more as a childhood rite of passage rather than the true nature of its destructive and aggressive manner.

Our society has indeed evolved since that time, and we now see bullying as a serious public health problem that exists both locally and globally. According to the 2014-15 school crime supplement of the National Center for Education Statistics and Bureau of Justice Statistics, approximately 21 percent of 12 to 18-year-old students experienced bullying nationwide. The American Psychological Association defines bullying as "a form of aggressive behavior in which someone intentionally and repeatedly causes another person injury or discomfort," and in which the "bullied individual typically has trouble defending him or herself and [has done] nothing to 'cause' the bullying." In order to be considered bullying, according to our government, the behavior must be aggressive and include an imbalance of power, be repetitious, or have the potential to happen more than once.

Bullying can take various forms, including verbal, social, physical, and cyberbullying. Verbal bullying can include teasing, name-calling, inappropriate sexual comments, taunting, and threatening to cause harm. Social bullying is a form of bullying in which someone's reputation or relationship is being deliberately harmed. This can include leaving someone out on purpose, telling other children not to be friends with someone, spreading rumors about someone, and embarrassing someone in public.

Physical bullying involves purposely hurting a person's body or possessions and can include hitting, kicking, pinching, spitting, tripping, pushing, taking or breaking someone's things, and making mean or rude hand gestures.

Cyberbullying is bullying through the use of electronic technological devices, such as cell phones, computers, and tablets. Cyberbullies communicate by way of social media sites, text messages, chatting, and websites. This form of bullying can include mean text messages and/or emails, rumors being spread by emails or posted on networking sites, and embarrassing pictures, videos, websites, and/or fake photos.

Bullying can happen to anyone and at any time, and risk factors do exist. Generally, children who are bullied have one or more of the following risk factors: they are perceived as being weak or unable to defend themselves, and they have low self-esteem, depression, or anxiety. They may have few friends, be less popular than the other children, and may not get along well with others. They may be perceived as being different from their peers, such as having weight issues, wearing glasses or different clothing, having a disability, or having a lesbian, gay, bisexual, or transgender sexual orientation.

On the other hand, children that are more likely to bully others are either well connected to or are more isolated from their peers. They tend to be aggressive or easily frustrated, think badly of others, have difficulty following rules, and/or have less parental involvement. They are more likely to view violence in a positive way and have friends who bully others. They tend to blame others for their problems and do not accept responsibility for their actions. They may get sent to the principal's office or to detention frequently, have unexplained extra money, or new belongings. They may be competitive and worry about their reputations or popularity.

Many warning signs may be present in someone who is affected by bullying, and it is imperative that we recognize these signs in order to take the appropriate action against bullying. Not all children who are bullied exhibit warning signs, but one should be aware of the following signs: unexplained injuries and lost or destroyed clothing, books, electronics, or jewelry. Bullied children may feel sick or fake illness, developing physical symptoms such as frequent headaches, stomachaches, difficulty sleeping, or nightmares. They may have sudden changes in eating habits, such as skipping meals or binge eating. They may not want to go to school and their grades may decline. They may feel helpless, sad, depressed, irritable, anxious, fearful, or angry. They may worry or have decreased self-esteem. They may have a sudden loss of friends, avoid social situations, run away from home, or harm themselves.

Bullying can lead to a wide range of health problems. Children and teenagers who are bullied, in addition to the above warning signs, may be physically injured by the perpetrator. Unhealthy behaviors of the bullied individual can develop and include smoking, substance and alcohol abuse, skipping school, neglecting schoolwork, getting into fights, running away from home, carrying a weapon to school, self-inflicted injuries such as cutting, and attempting suicide. Children and teenagers who bully others are also more likely to engage in unhealthy and risky behavior into adulthood. They are more likely to abuse alcohol and other drugs, drop out of school, get into fights, vandalize properties, engage in early sexual activity, have criminal convictions and traffic violations as adults, and be abusive toward their romantic partners, spouses, or children.

In order to help those who are bullied, we must first identify who is being bullied. According to statistics taken from the 2012 Indicators of School Crime and Safety, only in 40 percent of bullying incidents was an adult notified. Children and adolescents do not report bullying for fear of being rejected by their peers or fear of receiving more abuse from their perpetrator. They may feel helpless, socially isolated, or humiliated.

Once it is determined that bullying is occurring, one must take immediate action to intervene and respond consistently to bullying behavior. This sends a message to our youth that bullying is not acceptable. Adults should never ignore bullying behavior. This is a common mistake made by adults as they write it off to kids just being kids. Other common mistakes to avoid include the following: One should not try to sort out the facts immediately, force youth witnesses to say publicly what they saw, question the youth involved in front of other children, or force the children to apologize on the spot. The youth involved should be questioned separately and not together. Blame should not be placed on the child being bullied. The term "bullying" should not be used until it has been determined that a bullying event did occur. The police or medical personnel may need to be involved in certain situations.

After the bullying incident is resolved and all individuals are out of immediate danger, the next step is to determine the facts and determine if bullying did indeed occur. Other types of aggressive behavior, such as peer conflict and hazing, do not fit the definition of bullying and require different prevention and response strategies.

Commitments by teachers, school administrators, parents, and students are needed to help stop and prevent bullying. Teachers and school administrators must be observant and knowledgeable, involve students and parents as part of the solution, and set positive behavior expectations. Parents of bullied children need to be observant of the signs that their child is being bullied. They need to teach children how to handle being bullied and set appropriate boundaries with internet and phone technology. Parents of children who bully others need to educate their children about bullying and the harmful effects that it has on all involved. These parents need to avoid aggressive behavior or an overly strict environment in their homes, and they should address low self-esteem issues that may arise with their children. Students must do their part by reporting bullying and avoid bullying others themselves. We must all support the children involved in bullying.

The focus of this article has been on childhood bullying, but unfortunately bullying does occur in adulthood. I witnessed bullying during medical school, but I never interjected my frustration for fear that I would become the next victim. We see bullying in our offices, in politicians, in media, and in communistic countries. The ripple effect of bullying in our societal ponds is disruptive and devastating. We all must take a stance and protect our children and society from this harmful behavior.

CHINA HERITAGE TOUR

As a young adult, I never had the desire or vision to travel to an Eastern country. That all changed when my wife and I were making preparations to adopt our child. We both stepped on Chinese soil for the first time in 2007. Eleven years later, we found ourselves heading back to China. I am sharing with you my journal entries during our 2018 trip.

JUNE 9, 2018

It is 4 a.m. and I am sitting in the St. Louis airport waiting to board a plane to China. This June day already proves to be a hot, muggy, humidity-filled day, a stark contrast to the last time I traveled to China, which created the reason for my return trip today. Back on January 18, 2007, in the midst of the tragic ice storm in southwest Missouri, my friends and colleagues, Dr. David and Sarah Muegge, in the wee hours of the morning, traversed the dangerous and slick roads to take me and my wife to the Springfield-Branson National Airport. We were headed to China to bring our adopted daughter, then known as Feng Chao Ling, to her new home in America. Today my wife Angie, my daughter Rebecca Ling, and I are going on a Chinese Heritage Tour, thus allowing my daughter to step on her native soil for the first time since she was 14 months of age.

JUNE 10, 2018

We arrived in Beijing, China after a pleasant fourteen-hour flight from Toronto, Canada. We lost thirteen hours with the time difference, and we will regain these hours when we return home.

JUNE 11, 2018

In downtown Beijing, we walked about a mile to the south entrance of the Temple of Heaven Park and then entered the grounds of this ancient sacrificial complex through the Zhaoheng Gate. The Temple of Heaven was constructed from 1406 to 1420 during the reign of the Yongle Emperor of the Ming Dynasty. It is located in the southern part of Beijing, in the Chongwen District. The complex was built for emperors to worship heaven.

JUNE 12, 2018

We visited the Dragon Land Superior Jade Gallery in the Dengzhuang Changping District of Beijing, China. This jade factory is government regulated; this regulation guarantees that the jade is authentic, and the starting prices are set by the government.

We departed from the jade factory with our next destination being the Great Wall of China, at the Juyongguan section. The late Chairman Mao once said, "One is not truly a man until he has scaled the Great Wall." That being said, we all decided to conquer the Great Wall and so we traversed up some of the steep steps. The Juyongguan Great Wall section, thirty-seven miles from downtown Beijing at Juyong Pass, is the closest section from Beijing. At this location, one can view the ancient wall along with old tower and temple buildings. Juyong Pass encircles a valley, and it was the first of the three impregnable passes along the Great Wall. In ancient times, Juyong Pass was the northern direct access to Beijing.

We then headed to the China Center for Children's Welfare and Adoption. This place is special and of great significance to adopted parents of Chinese children. We were able to take a tour of the facility and see the "matching room," the actual place where a caseworker matched Rebecca Ling to me and Angie. After the tour, the children were given a Chinese culture class on how to do a traditional Chinese ink painting.

Our long but fun day ended with a traditional Peking duck dinner. We had several Chinese dishes to choose from along with the crispy and delicious Peking duck.

JUNE 13, 2018

We spent our morning at Tiananmen Square and the Forbidden City. Tiananmen Square, the largest square in the world, is located in the center of Beijing City. The square, which has a total area of 440,000 square meters, has held many ceremonies and demonstrations over the last hundred years. You may be most familiar with the 1989 protest in which a Chinese student faced off with Chinese military tanks. While in the square, you can visit Tiananmen Tower, Monument to the People's Heroes, Great Hall of the People, and Mao Zedong Memorial Hall, as well as see the national flag-raising ceremony. We were fortunate to be at the square during the changing of the guard ceremony, which occurs every two hours.

From the square, we walked underneath the road and arrived at Tiananmen, the Gate of Heavenly Peace. Tiananmen, first built in 1420 during the Ming Dynasty, is located north of Tiananmen Square. This monumental gate is used as a national symbol of China. The gate has held a portrait of the late General Mao since 1949. Each October 1, the portrait is replaced with an identical reproduction, to commemorate the anniversary of the founding of the People's Republic of China. A lot of people mistake Tiananmen to be part of the Forbidden City, but actually it is the gate to the Forbidden City.

After walking through the Gate of Heavenly Peace, we entered the Forbidden City, now known as the Palace Museum. The Forbidden City, built between 1406 and 1420, is the world's largest palace complex, covering over 180 acres, consisting of 980 buildings. It served until 1911 as the imperial palace for twenty-four emperors during the Ming and Qing Dynasties.

After leaving the Forbidden City, we took a short bus ride to the Hutong area for lunch with a local family, and we also enjoyed a rickshaw ride and a walking tour. Hutong is the name given to a small street or lane that originated during the Yuan Dynasty. At one time, there were thirty-six Hutong areas, but now there is only one Hutong area left with around four hundred courtyards. We took a rickshaw to lunch at the home of the Fang family. We had the rare opportunity to enter into the home of one of the Hutong inhabitants, where Ms. Fang served us a local meal. It was delicious and we were so grateful for her hospitality. After lunch, we had a guided walking tour of the area and finished the walking tour at the home of a famous local artist.

JUNE 14, 2018

After flying to Chengdu, we were transported to Wangjianglou Park. Chengdu is the capital city of the Sichuan Province of China. The city has over 16 million people, and it is a favorite location for Chinese retirees. Wangjianglou Park is one of many parks in the city where the locals go for leisure and relaxation. We ended our day by walking around the park and having jasmine tea at the tea house in the park. Angie and I both received shoulder massages from a local woman, and Angie even opted to get an ear massage.

JUNE 15, 2018

At Chengdu Panda Reserve, we spent the first hour walking around watching pandas play and eat. The weather was perfect to visit the reserve, as it had just rained and cooled the air. Pandas are playful and active in cooler weather. Our family then participated in the optional panda photo. We suited up in blue jumpsuits, gloves, and shoe covers and then walked to a different section of the reserve. While the attendants distracted the panda with food, we sat next to her for photographs. Our panda was 1 1/2 years old and weighed about 225 pounds. The Chinese people regard the panda as a symbol of peace, harmony, and friendship.

After lunch, we headed back to downtown Chengdu for shopping at Jinli Street. Jinli Street, located to the east of the Wuhou Temple, was one of the busiest commercial areas during the Shu Kingdom (221-263 BC). The street was restored in 2004 and opened back to the public. The narrow street has on both sides old-world stores, teahouses, food shops, and hotels. The street is modeled on the architectural style of a traditional western Sichuan Province town from the Qing Dynasty.

We ended our evening by attending the Legend of Face Changing show at the Shufeng Yayun Sichuan Opera House in downtown Chengdu. Sichuan Opera, originated in Chengdu, is a beautiful art form that features mask changing and fire spitting tricks.

JUNE 16, 2018

We just boarded our high speed "bullet" train from Chengdu, Sichuan, China to Xi'an, Shaanxi, China. Now I am sitting in a train that is moving at over 200 miles per hour. The train is quiet and smooth, unlike the rocking motion of the slower trains that we have back home. The scenery is calming with rice paddies and mountains.

Before arriving at our hotel, we diverted our attention to Xi'an's Ancient City Wall. This wall was erected in the fourteenth century during the Ming Dynasty, under the regimen of Emperor Zhu Yuanzhang. The fortification wall was built as a military defense system to protect the city. The wall is nine miles in length and surrounds the inner city of Xi'an. A moat runs along the outside of the wall. There are four gates, north, west, east, and south, along the wall, as well as ninety-eight flanking towers, with one located every 120 meters. The wall is as wide as a road, and visitors enjoy riding bikes and flying kites on top of the wall.

JUNE 17, 2018

We visited the government sanctioned Xi'an Hande Artwork Factory where we were able to purchase replicated terracotta warriors. We then ventured to the museum to see the actual terracotta warriors. This phenomenal archeological site was discovered on March 29, 1974, by farmers digging a well. It was unknown to the world for over 2,200 years. The discovery area is in the Lintong District of Xi'an in Shaanxi Province of the People's Republic of China. It is the largest pottery figurine group ever found in China. The terracotta sculptures represent the armies of the first emperor of China, Qin Shi Huang. The purpose of this endeavor, utilizing over 700,000 workers, was to have an army to protect the emperor during his afterlife. If the servants did not die during the process of this massive construction, then they were massacred as human sacrifices upon completion of this project. There are over 8,000 life-sized sculptures, of which 2,000 have been uncovered and reconstructed. After another family-style lunch at the museum's restaurant, we then departed Xi'an.

JUNE 18, 2018

We just finished a four-hour boat cruise down the Lijiang River from Guilin to Yangshuo. Along the way we saw goats, cattle, ducks, and water buffalo. We were able to also see riverside villages, but the most spectacular view was the mountain range. I recall seeing these mountains in a magazine as a youth and I envisioned a far-off, exotic land. The backside of the 20 yuan Chinese currency note has a view of the Guilin mountain range scenery. We were able to have this exact view from our cruise.

JUNE 19, 2018

After a morning tai chi class along the riverbank, we headed back to Guilin, with a stop at a pearl factory along the way.

Well, it is 9:15 p.m. here in Guilin, and our group tour has come to an end. We had a wonderful time spending the last few hours together as a group. We had a family-style meal and then some of the children showed off their talents with song, dance, and magic. Ling chose to sing *Amazing Grace*, and she brought down the house.

June 21, 2018

We are in ChaoHu City in Anhui Province. I am flooded with mixed emotions—a fear of what could have been, a joy for what is, and an unconditional love I have for my dear sweet child. I choose to leave out most of the details of our orphanage visit, as the time we spent was an intimate family moment. I burst into tears when I met and was able to thank in person the woman who saved my daughter's life and for whom my daughter is named.

June 22, 2018

We are staying at the Jin Jiang Tower in Downtown Shanghai, China. This city is massive with over 24 million people.

Last night was a fantastic way to end our China tour. I booked a tour through Viator titled "VIP Huangpu River Cruise and Shanghai Lights Private Evening Tour." Our tour guide picked us up last evening at 6:30 p.m. and drove us to Shanghai Old Town. This area, located in the southeast region of the city center, houses many historic buildings. You can contrast these buildings to the high-rise modern buildings seen in the distance. The Old Town buildings now house restaurants, food shops, souvenir shops, teahouses, and jewelry and clothing stores. It is a favorite spot for both locals and visitors. Old Town also has an active temple along with the Nine-Zigzag Bridge and many other buildings that are significant to the Chinese people.

After our walking excursion at Shanghai Old Town, we then headed to the Huangpu River for a river boat cruise. We enjoyed VIP class tickets and were thus able to avoid the long boarding lines. Once aboard the yacht, we were escorted to our own enclosed luxurious room in the front of the boat.

While on the cruise, even though it was raining, we are able to enjoy the famous Shanghai skyline. In the summertime from 7 until 10 p.m. (and starting at 6 p.m. in the wintertime), downtown Shanghai lights up its skyscraper buildings. We were also able to see the colonial-era buildings alongside the Bund.

Finally, we headed to the Pudong Lujiazui Commercial and Business Area, where we were able to see many highrise buildings that were built in the last twenty years. We had the opportunity to stand at the base of China's tallest building and the second largest building in the world. It is designed to look like a dragon as it twists upward.

After our three-and-a-half-hour excursion, our guide then drove us back to our hotel, which is in the French Concession area of Shanghai. The Shanghai French Concession was a foreign concession from 1849 until 1943. There was also the British Concession and the American Concession, which consolidated to become the Shanghai International Settlement.

Most Americans don't think of China as a tourist destination. However, this country should certainly be placed on one's travel bucket list.

COLLEGE LIFE

I am going to preface this topic with the fact that I attended college from 1983 through 1987 and medical school from 1992 through 1996. Though it has been several years since I have attended college, I am well versed to write about what college life meant to me. I also feel that my experiences are still relevant to the college student and aspiring college student today. While not everyone has the desire or the ability to attend college, many adolescents and adults will choose to enroll in higher education. That being said, my goal is to show the reader the value that college life has on the individual and society as a whole.

I thoroughly enjoyed my preparation and attendance of college. The basis and foundation for college life today have not changed since I graduated from St. Mary's University of San Antonio, Texas in 1987. Sure, technology has advanced, with laptops and tablets replacing heavy and bulky textbooks. Not to mention online classes and degrees are now being offered to students. But the goal for the student to expand their knowledge base is still the same.

For the college-bound student, determining where to attend college is an exciting time. Back when I was looking at colleges, I had guidance only from my school counselor, college sports teams, college fairs, reference books, and word of mouth in knowing the existence of a specific college. These days, the internet opens up a plethora of information to the college seeker. Unfortunately, many colleges have become cost prohibitive for some, as college tuitions have skyrocketed over the last thirty years. Scholarships and financial aid assistance are more important now than ever. College preparation is, however, beyond the scope of this article. We will assume that the student has done the appropriate work, been accepted into a college, and is able to afford their chosen school.

The main goal for attending college should be to attain knowledge. This may or may not result in a college degree. The course work can be done by attending classes in person, online, or through a combination of both. For many college graduates, the goal is to be able to enter into a specific field or to advance their already-established career. Some people choose to get a basic liberal arts education, then go on to focus on their career with an advanced degree.

For the in-class student, one must decide if they are going to commute to college classes or live on campus. Many colleges now mandate that college freshmen live on campus, unless they have extenuating circumstances that prevent on-campus living. This decision can be influenced by many factors. These factors can include part-time or full-time enrollment status, as well as the student's age, marital status, financial situation, and work status.

Assuming that the student has the ability and option to live on campus, I strongly encourage that they consider this option. I have attended college both as a commuter and as a student living on campus. For me, commuting to college seemed more like a chore, and I was just glad to be done with the day. I had to spend extra energy to participate in extracurricular activities as a commuter. I feel like I missed out on opportunities that would have been available to me if I had lived on campus.

When I attended St. Mary's University, I lived on campus from my freshman year until I graduated with my bachelor's degree. Students living on campus have an entirely different experience than those who commute. I believe that a large chunk of one's college education is attained by campus living. Students learn how to be more independent and communicate better. They also have easier access to college services and activities than the commuters. They are surrounded by people with similar goals and others with different upbringings and cultures. They have more time to devote to their studies, they are able to expand their social base, and they feel part of a wider community. Growing up in the inner city of St. Louis, I have fond memories of staying up late, chatting with dorm friends about their life on a farm or in a different country. By living on campus, I was able to grow as a person, and I felt better connected to the world. If they are able to do so, I enthusiastically encourage college students to live on campus.

Time management is a very important skill to have, and you must learn it in order to have a successful college career. In college, school bells do not ring, and the students are responsible for their own time. Balancing class time with homework, free time, extracurricular activities, eating, sleeping, and any jobs that the student may have becomes so crucial in college. Excellent time management in college sets the student up for a more prosperous and enjoyable life for years to come.

It is often said that college life is the best time of a person's life. I disagree with this statement in that I believe life is what you make it. Now in my fifties, I am as happy as I was when I was attending college. However, I did feel the freest when I was in college. I have fond memories of my college days and I would not trade my time there for anything.

My family and I recently were driving around Southern Illinois University at Edwardsville for the first time. We were able to drive around one of the largest campuses with all the beautiful foliage and landscapes. We witnessed college students moving into the dorms for the upcoming school year. I was happy for them, knowing that many of them will have enjoyable and rewarding days in the weeks and months ahead. In a few years, I look forward to living those days again vicariously through my daughter, as she will start planning for her college days.

MEDICAL NOVEL REVIEWS

In order to keep our mind, spirit, and body in balance, physicians need diversions from medicine, just like other people with their chosen profession. One of my diversions is reading. When I have the time, usually while I am working out, I read one of my wife's thriller novels that she has on her Nook. But sometimes I find myself reading books that have a medical theme. You would think this would be counterproductive to the balancing concept, but ironically, this seems to enhance mine. Reading about non-technical medical topics confirms for me why I went into the medical field and helps me keep my sanity. Here are five of my favorite medically related books that you should consider putting on your reading list.

Most of us older physicians remember the days when we had hospital rounds, delivered babies, visited the nursing homes, and even made house calls. Back in the 1990s, when I was practicing in rural mid-Missouri, I covered two nursing homes and made house calls to my homebound patients every Wednesday and whenever the need arose. The book *House Calls and Hitching Posts* is a refreshing reminder of those busy but seemingly simpler days. This book is a chronicle of short stories about Dr. Elton

Lehman's thirty-six years of practicing medicine in rural Ohio among the Amish. His stories are a wonderful and enlightening reflection of how our humanity comes into play with our medical duties. At a time when our medical field seems so fragmented and humanity seems to be playing second fiddle, reading this book will remind the reader why medicine is a worthy profession.

I have never been in the military. I have never experienced war. I did not grow up in the 1940s, nor did I grow up in the South. So, when my attending physician during my family medicine rotation in Savannah, Georgia, said that I should read *When All the World Was Young* by Ferrol Sams, I balked at the idea. A year later, when I found myself matched at Memorial Medical Center and thus headed back to Savannah, Georgia, I thought I'd better listen to my new boss. The book, though fiction, captures the essence of the South through the eyes of Surgical Technician PFC Porter Osborne. The author, a physician himself, is able to effectively pull you into the story. Having completed my residency in Georgia, I could relate to the stories of Grady Memorial Hospital in Atlanta and Mercer University in Macon. But even for those readers who have never touched foot in Georgia, this book will broaden your mind.

Since graduating from the University of Missouri School of Medicine in Columbia, Missouri, I have become enamored by the history of the university. So I was excited when a comprehensive book on the topic was published by one of my medical school instructors. The late Dr. Hugh Stephenson published *Aesculapius Was a Mizzou Tiger: An Illustrated History of Medicine at Ol' Mizzou* back in 1998. Though over twenty years have passed since this book was published, it is still a relevant reference source. Do not be fooled by the book's title or cover photo, as the book is packed with over a thousand pages of interesting historical data and information relating to my alma mater. In my opinion, every Mizzou medical school graduate and those practicing medicine in Missouri should have this book on their coffee table.

Sometimes, we only have a few minutes to spare. It is nice to sit down and read a few pages of a book without having to stop in the middle of a chapter. The book *On Doctoring*, edited by physicians, is a compilation of short stories, essays, and poems related to the practice of medicine. It is an inspiring collection of works that masterfully capture the trials, triumphs, and tribulations of our profession. This book is interesting both for the medical and non-medical professional.

By the time I was in the internship of my medical residency program, I was already burned out with medicine. I was so embarrassed and ashamed of my emotions and how I sometimes viewed my patients that I was ready to quit medicine altogether. I was emotionally, mentally, and physically drained, and I was just starting out in medicine. My future looked bleak, and I was surely second-guessing my career decision. Then I met a colleague who reminded me that I was human, that my feelings were normal under the circumstances, and that my black clouds would eventually dissipate and open into clear skies. To reiterate his comments, he suggested that I read *The House of God*. The book is repulsive, vulgar, and shocking. Yet I believe that it saved my life and my medical career. Medical training used to be dehumanizing, demoralizing, and engulfed with psychological scarring. Times have fortunately changed for the better in regard to our profession's method of training young physicians. Sam Shems, a physician himself, was able to capture in words what we older physicians endured during our training.

I hope you enjoyed reading about one of my diversions. I have read several medically related books in my days, but I have found these to be the most interesting for me. I also believe that these books will help close the gap that exists between laypeople and those in the medical field. So after finishing reading this book, head on over to the bookstore or the library and open up one of the noted books. I'm confident that you will not be disappointed.

RESOLUTIONS

January is the month of resolutions, a.k.a. a New Year's opportunity. The origin and transformation of our New Year's resolution tradition are interesting, even though the vast majority of those making resolutions fail in achieving their goals.

The Babylonians, over four thousand years ago, were thought to be the first group of people who made New Year's resolutions. Their new year began in mid-March, when crops were planted, at which time they held Akitu, a twelve-day religious festival. They made promises (resolutions) to the gods that they would pay off their debts as well as return any items that they borrowed. The Babylonians believed that by keeping these promises, their gods would grant good fortune to them for the coming year. However, if they did not keep their promises, then they would fall out of the gods' favor, resulting in very bad fortune.

In 46 B.C., Julius Caesar established January 1 as the beginning of the new year. January was named after Janus, a two-faced Roman god whose spirit inhabited doorways and arches. This deity possessed the ability to see all things past and future, thus the reason for the two faces. Because of this ability, the Romans offered sacrifices and made promises of goodwill to Janus and sought to keep them for the coming year.

In 1582, when Pope Gregory XIII introduced his Gregorian calendar, he maintained January 1 as the start of the new year. Over time, the New Year's resolutions became integrated into Christian traditions. The first day of the new year was a renewal time for Christians to reflect on their past mistakes, while resolving to become better Christians in the future. In 1740, the founder of Methodism, John Wesley, created the Covenant Renewal Service. This service, also known as Watch Night Service, was commonly held on New Year's Eve or New Year's Day. New Year's celebrations often were wild and rowdy. The Watch Night Service came to be a spiritual alternative with hymn singing, praying, and readings from scriptures.

Today our New Year's resolutions have morphed into a predominantly secular practice. What once started out as promises to the gods is now purely focused on self-improvement. Over 40 percent of Americans make New Year's resolutions, but only 17 percent commit to them, and 9 percent succeed in achieving their goals.

The most popular New Year's resolutions include the following: eat a healthier diet and lose weight, quit smoking, make better financial decisions, exercise more, learn a new hobby, spend more time with family, find a romantic partner, find a better job, read more, reduce stress, travel, and live life to the fullest. Getting healthy and fit seem to top the list year after year.

Most of the people attempting resolutions fail because they either take on an enormous task, do not have the knowledge or understanding to make successful changes, or were not truly committed to their goals. As a physician, I am well versed with the Stages of Change Model and the S.M.A.R.T. goals. Not only is it a good idea for me to periodically review these concepts; it is also important for the general public to understand and implement them in their lives.

The Transtheoretical Model, also known as the Stages of Change Model, was developed by psychologists James O. Prochaska and Carlo Di Clemente. This model shows how individuals move through six stages of change: precontemplation, contemplation, preparation, action, maintenance, and termination.

In the precontemplation stage, people, for various reasons, have no intention to make changes. I often hear that around Thanksgiving time; patients will state they are not even going to try to make any changes until maybe the New Year. Fortunately, some clever wellness group came up with the "Maintain, Don't Gain" challenge. This allows us to help these individuals get through the gluttonous holiday season with less damage and more control and stability.

With the contemplation stage, people have the intention to make changes within the next six months. They are aware that their current behavior may be adversely affecting their own well-being. The new year propels a lot of people into this and the next stage. As health care providers, this is where our intervention, suggestions, and support can help advance them into the other stages.

The third stage is the preparation stage, where people are starting to make changes and take action within the next thirty days. They are in the process of developing their plan of action, such as seeing a counselor or joining a gym.

The action stage is where people have changed their behavior within the last six months and have the intention to progress forward with their behavioral change. For example, they may have quit smoking or lost excess weight.

The fifth stage is the maintenance stage, in which people have sustained their behavioral change for over six months. They intend to continue on their current trajectory and work to avoid relapsing to the earlier stages.

The final stage, though rarely reached or discussed, is the termination stage, in which people are absolutely sure that they will not relapse. The individual can exit and re-enter at any stage, and a relapse can occur in any of the first five stages listed. These stages of change can occur at any time of the year, though our society sees a mass number enter them around the new year. It is important to know the stage that our patients are in so that we can give them the appropriate support measures.

Once people have decided to make healthy behavioral changes in their lives, they need the tools and skills to be successful. George Doran, Arthur Miller, and James Cunningham published an article in the November 1981 issue of *Management Review* titled "There's a S.M.A.R.T. Way to Write Management Goals and Objectives." These goals were originally used as a business tool as a means to improve project management processes.

S.M.A.R.T is an acronym that initially stood for **S**pecific, **M**easurable, **A**ssignable, **R**ealistic, and **T**ime Based. Over time, the healthcare industry adapted these goals into **S**pecific, **M**easurable, **A**ttainable/**A**ccountable, **R**ealistic/ **R**elevant, and **T**ime Specific.

A Specific goal significantly improves the chance that the goal will be accomplished. An example of that is setting a goal to lose weight. Rather than just stating weight-loss as a goal, one says that they will lose thirty pounds of weight over the next three months at two to three pounds per week.

The goal needs to be Measurable. By keeping track of one's progress, one is able to stay on task and reach their target goals and dates.

The goal needs to be Attainable and Accountable. Breaking the goal down into steps that lead to the desired result will allow one to attain the incremental steps and also be accountable to the process.

The goal needs to be Realistic and Relevant. Far too many New Year's resolutions are unrealistic, unattainable goals. Steps should be relevant in achieving the goal, such as reducing caloric intake and increasing activity in order to lose weight.

The goal needs to be Time Specific. A clearly defined time frame with a target or deadline date needs to be made.

As a medical professional, I have the responsibility to assist my patients in their needs to live a healthy life in mind, spirit, and body. Though some amount of intervention should be done at every visit, the new year is a perfect opportunity for me to engage my patients to live life to the fullest.

Snow Day

When I was a child, all the way up until my teenage years, I was always excited when the school weekday would turn into a snow day. In elementary school, my twin brother and I would watch the news, eagerly awaiting the weather portion of the newscast. Back then, there was no such thing as weather apps. We also did not have the luxury of the internet, where we could instantaneously find out this information. As time passed, the news stations eventually announced school closings by having them scroll on the bottom of the television screen. School closings would be listed alphabetically. We would impatiently wait to see if our school was listed. Sometimes the listings would be disrupted by a commercial. We would then have to sit through the commercial only to discover that the school listings started again from the beginning.

Often we would go to bed not knowing if our school would be closed the next day. We would wake up early, quickly turn on the radio, and listen intently for any additional school closings. For some reason, back in the 1970s, a blizzard would be needed for us to get our snow day. But living in St. Louis, our wish would often come true, and the eight-inch snowfall the night before would shutter our school the next day.

Being a gambler by nature, I would gamble on my school studies in light of a potential snow day. If I had homework or a test the next day and it looked like our school would be closed for a snow day, I would sometimes take the chance and let my studying lapse the night before. The exhilaration and, frankly, relief of hearing those glorious words that my school was closed for the day were worth the gamble. Sometimes, fate would not be in my favor, and I would find myself scrambling to complete my homework or cram for a test that I had hoped I wouldn't be taking that day. On the other hand, I was so disappointed when I had completed a project or studied for a test only to find out that the project's deadline or test would be delayed due to school closing for the day. As I grew up, I came to realize that completing the task itself was reward enough.

If you lived in the top half of the United States, chances are you experienced a snow day while growing up. One memorable time was on a winter weekend in the 1970s, when over a foot of snow fell onto our city. We woke up on a Sunday morning with snow still falling from the sky. This was the snowfall of snowfalls, and we just knew the impact that it would have on our school week. We managed to be off school for the entire week that year, and it was ever so joyful. Of course, that didn't stop my father from fulfilling our religious responsibilities.

My parents, being devout Catholics, were not going to miss mass that Sunday morning. With over a foot of snowfall on the ground and streets, our city was immobilized and everything came to a halt. We were not able to drive to church, which was about a mile from our home. Heck, we couldn't even get the garage door open, as it was stuck to the ground. So our family bundled up with the appropriate clothing, and we headed out to mass. It took us almost an hour to trudge the mile to our destination. But the journey was truly incredible and unforgettable. As we walked through the middle of the streets, we found ourselves in the midst of a winter wonderland. Snow glistened on the trees, and the sidewalks and streets disappeared as if they were lost under the carpet of snow. No one was outside, and it gave us the feeling that we were the last four people on this Earth. When we finally arrived at church, the priest greeted all of the twelve people that made it to mass, and said if it were him, he would have stayed home. Really? That was his response? At that moment, I wished I had just stayed home. But the adventure we had that morning was a memory that I will take to my grave.

The good thing about a snow day is that it brought out a prosperous zest in many of us young entrepreneurs. Just a few inches would put us in business, but the higher the snowfall, the better the payout. Equipped with our snow wear and a snow shovel, and of course after shoveling our own driveway, my brother and I would head out to the neighborhood. We would do a cold-call presentation to our potential customers as we offered to shovel their sidewalk and driveway for an agreed-upon fee. Initially, we let the customer set the price, and then as we became more experienced, we would let the market dictate our fees. Sometimes, a negotiation would take place, and then we would get to work. We would always end our day with a lucrative investment and fat wallets tucked in our pants pockets.

Another memorable snow day was when I was attending college at St. Mary's University in San Antonio, Texas. I suspect that most Texans have never experienced a snow day, but that would change for a lot of Texas school children in 1985. It was January 1985, and my brother and I had just returned to San Antonio for the spring semester. A snowstorm of the century was brewing in south central Texas. That semester, there were about a hundred of us St. Mary's students from the St. Louis area. So when the snow started to fall in the middle of the night, many of the Texas students woke us "Yankees" up in order to show them how to play in the snow. With most of us only having light jackets and using socks for gloves, we all went out to the field and played touch football in the snow. Tackling was sometimes involved, but no one was injured as the abundance of snow cushioned our fall.

Our friend and schoolmate was flying in from St. Louis that weekend, and we were given the task of picking him up at the airport. By the time we arrived at the airport, we learned that all flights had been canceled except for his flight. Rumor was that the airport had only one de-icer and that they had to improvise on clearing the runway. As we looked out the huge windows onto the runway, our mouths dropped in astonishment. Almost all available vehicles of various types were in a line going up and down the runway. We were told that was their plan to melt the snow that accumulated on the main runway. We all gasped in relief as our friend's plane landed and came to a screeching halt safely grounded. Over thirteen inches of snow fell onto the streets of San Antonio, Texas, that weekend. The next day, the mayor shut down the city and instructed all San Antonians to shelter in place; the city experienced a citywide snow day.

That was the last of my personal snow days, and I thought I would not experience one again, that is, until I married a teacher. My wife is a middle-grade teacher. After moving back to Missouri with me, she was so excited when the weather developed for a potential snow day. You would think that children are the only ones grateful for snow days, but teachers take the cake. They seem to me to be ever so thankful for that unscheduled day off of school. So, there I was, finding myself watching the news with my wife, yearning for her wish to come true.

My daughter was fortunate enough to experience the joy of a snow day, but soon, in the near future, snow days will come to an end and only be memories for those that were lucky enough to have experienced them. As school districts across our land develop their infrastructures for online learning, snow days will become extinct. So, if you ever get the opportunity to have a snow day, make sure you experience it to the fullest, as it just may be the last one ever.

COMPUTERS AND THE INTERNET

The personal computer was made available to the general public in 1974. When I was a child, I remember my uncle having one in his home. When our family would visit his house, I would beg for him to rev it up so we could watch him work on a real, live computer. He wouldn't let us use it, but that was OK, as we were simply mesmerized by being in the same room as this marvelous piece of electronics. My memory has somewhat faded, but I remember the screen being about four inches wide with a black background. A green underscore would flash on the screen. My uncle would peck out a few taps on the keyboard, and voila, letters would appear on the screen. I would not have that intimate of an experience with a personal computer again until high school.

As I type on this laptop computer, I recall a time in the early 1980s while I was attending college; I was still without a personal computer. The cost of a personal computer at that time was a few thousand dollars. My classmates and I couldn't afford a computer of our own. As a result, we had to rely on the now archaic methods available at that time. Fortunately for me, I had one of those fancy electric typewriters. Not only that, but when I made an error, I could pop in a correction ribbon cartridge rather than having to start all over. One stressor back then in college was typing up a paper the night before, finding out the ink cartridge was dry, and then rushing to the store before it closed in order to get a replacement.

By 1987, I purchased my first personal computer, an Apple Macintosh. At that time, I was working as a research assistant at Washington University in St. Louis. Being a part of the college staff, I was able to secure my first computer at a significantly discounted price. I became obsessed with that computer, and I spent a lot of my free time on it, watching as the screen glowed in my darkened room. Thankfully, I did manage to be more productive with it once the novelty wore off.

Fast-forward thirty-plus years, and computers are now everywhere; they have been integrated into almost every aspect of our lives. We have our personal computers as desktops, laptops, and tablets. We have computers in our security systems, appliances, automobiles, and even some furniture. Our phones and watches are even computerized. Today, I can do a Dick Tracy, and talk on my watch. *Dick Tracy* was an American comic strip based on a detective with the same name; it debuted back in 1931. In 1946, Detective Tracy's two-way radio wristwatch became a recognizable icon. Even as recent as the 1990s, a watch phone was only a fantasy. It wasn't until 2015, when the Apple Watch was introduced, that it became a common accessory.

My mother and my in-laws can tell you about a time when no area homes had televisions or how they had to live without indoor plumbing. I can only go back so far with memories of no remote control. That was prehistoric enough, and to imagine life again without computers ... well, I don't want to even think about it.

When one thinks about computers, the internet automatically seems to come to mind. Speaking of caveman days, I can recall a time when I lived without the internet, or so I thought. Rumors existed back in the 1990s that a United States vice president invented the internet, and I can recall a commercial where the advertisement showed someone reaching the end of the internet. The birth of the internet, albeit in a primitive form, was delivered in 1969, by the Advanced Research Projects Agency Network (ARPANET). As technology advanced, Transmission Control Protocol and Internet Protocol, or TCP/IP, became the standard communications model for data transmission between multiple networks. By 1990, the World Wide Web was invented, thereby allowing the user to access data online via websites and hyperlinks.

Let's recall what life was like without the internet. One thing that comes to mind is having to lug out those huge, bulky white pages and Yellow Pages. The white and Yellow Pages were collections of personal and business telephone numbers and addresses respectively. Back in the 1970s, if you wanted to make a merchandise purchase, one option was to get in your car and travel all the way to the store hoping they would have what you were looking for. Or you could get on the phone and call the various businesses listed in the Yellow Pages. It could be a tedious process, and sometimes you would end up empty handed. These days, you can open an app on your phone or tablet or search the web, and within minutes, you would have multiple choices for purchase. It could be purchased locally, sent by mail order, or even both.

Remember trying to accumulate large amounts of information before surfing the internet? You had to trudge on over to the library or a bookstore or pull out large encyclo-pedias, if you had a set. After spending several hours work-ing on your search, you then had to collect the informa-tion, often like a scavenger hunt, and then carry the heavy load home. These days, the astute researcher can extract the information of interest within minutes from the inter-net. All the research can be stored on one's phone or com-puter, so the weight of your load was the same as when you started, since fortunately the added data doesn't add any weight to your device.

We mainly think of the internet as a means to view web-sites or collect data, but the internet is now integrated in the majority of our lives. The internet's tentacles have wrapped themselves around our daily lives so tightly that we would be hard pressed to untangle them. Most people's work duties involve interacting in some way with the inter-net. Our systems of transportation, defense, engineering, communications, commerce, medicine, and many others rely on the internet. One can certainly live off the grid, but it would take preparation, a certain strength, and a true commitment to do so. In any case, we all should take peri-odic breaks from the internet grid to balance our mind, body, and soul.

I CLOSED MY EYES AND WHAT DID I SEE

Have you ever wondered what life would be like if you suddenly lost your vision? Unfortunately for millions of people, living without that sense is their everyday reality. I do not desire to become blind or wish that upon anyone else. Many individuals who have developed blindness probably would like to have their vision back. Those born without this basic sense do not miss it as they were never aware of it in the first place. Others will tell you that becoming blind was a godsend and helped define who they are. It is true that when you take away one of the basic senses, the other senses go into hyperdrive and become more adaptable to one's environment.

I believe that in order to totally understand people's perspective, you need to walk in their shoes for a while. I'm not saying that you have to become blind to understand the blind, go to war to understand the soldier, or have a child to understand the parent. While it is true that a full appreciation of one's perspective comes only from experiencing that person's perspective, all of us can show love and empathy without having to have the same experiences. That being said, I sat down in the comfort of my chair this morning and closed my eyes, and this is what I saw.

The first thing I notice is the whirling, buzzing sound of something in the distance. The sound is oscillating on and off in order to keep its contents cool. As I sit in the living room, I know that our kitchen is located behind me. I become content in knowing that our refrigerator is doing the job it was meant to do.

I can hear a clicking sound behind me and then a whooshing sound around me. It is a hot, summer morning and the house, like the refrigerator, is also trying to keep its contents cool. Within minutes, I can feel the air around me drop in temperature as it whisks by and onto my legs. I am happy to come to realize that the air conditioner is also working properly.

I don't hear anything above me really until I zone in on that area of the house. The cool crispness of the air-conditioned air is being pushed onto my skin like the gentle breeze that I have experienced outside on a windy day. The humming sound of the ceiling fan high above my head is ever so faint.

As I move around in my chair, I can hear the squeaking sound underneath me. My hands feel the smoothness of the furniture's material. Since I am shirtless, I hear a sucking, peeling sound as I pull my trunk from the back of the chair. The rubbing sound is all too familiar as I lay my head back on the cushion, knowing that my trusty old leather recliner is still supporting me well.

I can hear chirping coming from near my window and, every so often, what seems to be like a beautiful short repetitive song. The sounds are garbled and jumbled. I recognize that sound, as I suspect it is from one of the finches that fly about and live in my backyard.

The natural beauty of the bird sounds is soothing to my mind. Then, I hear something not so natural, something artificially made, that disrupts the finches' calls. At first the sound is a cacophonous interruption, but then I recognize it and appreciate it for its purpose.

My mind starts to wander about where the jet plane is taking its passengers as it passes by my house high above the sky. I think of the last time I was riding in a plane and how this has been the longest since I have flown in one.

Suddenly I am pulled back to reality from the woofing and barking coming from our bedroom. Two of our three dogs, a black Lab mix and an American Staffordshire terrier mix, have decided it is time to get up. They are letting my wife know that they are ready to go outside to explore and do their business. Within seconds, a high-pitched screeching bark erupts from behind me. I hear my daughter telling our third dog, a miniature pinscher mix, to stop barking. A creaking sound occurs as my daughter's bedroom door is opened and the pitter-patter sound is made as the dog's claws tap on the wooden floor underneath her feet. Her yipping sound soon fades as I hear the sliding sound of our glass door being opened and closed.

I start to notice the various scents that fill the air. I can smell the sweet whiff of the vanilla coconut foam soap that I washed my hands with earlier this morning. The air is also mixed with a freshness, as the house was recently cleaned. Yet I also sense a greasy smell from the chicken that was cooked for dinner last night.

I finally open my eyes. My exercise of being in the moment was relaxing, uplifting, and successful. I know you probably thought that this section was about the blind, and in a way it is, but I will leave those without the sense of sight to tell their own story. But if you don't live in the moment, you will become blind to the present.

A CONNECTED WORLD

I believe that we, as humans, are all connected and that everything we do in our lives has either beneficial or consequential effects to the world's energy. I may seem to be spouting off some Eastern philosophy on life, but let's take a realistic stroll into the snapshots of people's lives and see how we truly are all connected.

Jackie was having a very difficult day. She had just come from work, where she was getting overburdened with the daily grind of her duties. She had personal bills to pay, and they seemed to be collecting exponentially. Her relationship with her boyfriend was rocky, and they were on the verge of a breakup. Her life seemed to be unraveling, and she was desperately looking to reverse her downward spiral. She felt like nothing was going her way, and she needed a positive sign in her life.

Joe was having a great day. He just sealed a deal on a multi-million-dollar property he was selling, and he would soon be receiving a fat commission. He was sitting in the drive-thru waiting for his freshly brewed coffee, when the barista told him that the car in front of him had bought his drink. Exhilarated with this small act of kindness, he also decided to pay it forward. Never knowing his recipient, he felt content when he drove off after paying the bill for the car behind him.

Jackie decided she needed a pick-me-up drink, with caffeine and a powerful jolt, in order to snap her out of her funky mood. As she pulled up to the drive-thru pay window, she realized that she had left her purse, with her wallet in it, at work. She would have to apologize to the barista and embarrassingly skulk away from the building. But to her surprise, the barista instead gave her the drink, informed her that the guy in front of her had paid for it, and wished her a great day. Jackie thanked God that, for that moment, her silver cloud had dissipated, and a ray of sunshine reflected off her face.

Tom was inside the coffee shop when he heard about what was transpiring outside in the drive-thru line. As he left the building, he thought about how he didn't have the time or the money to participate in such frivolous deeds. Not paying attention to his surroundings, he bumped into a man as he was leaving, spilling his drink all over the man's shirt. He apologized but didn't really mean it as he felt the blame was on the man for getting in his way.

Tom was crossing the street, not paying attention to his environment, when a car seemed to have come out of nowhere. The car was exiting the coffee shop's drive thru. Tom was struck on his left hip, and he landed on his right side. He ended up striking his head on the pavement, which left him unconscious.

Joe was on a high as he sped away from the coffee shop. He was changing the channel on his radio station, when suddenly and without warning, he felt an impact on the front of his car. He hit the brakes, got out of his car, and his worst fear was realized, as an adult man lay unconscious in the middle of the road. Joe fortunately recalled his basic life-support training course that he took last summer. He quickly took action, stabilized the man, and waited until the ambulance arrived to transport the man to the hospital.

Jackie's uncle, Dr. Tanner, was on staff as an emergency medicine physician at the hospital nearby. Her Aunt Lilly, Dr. Tanner's wife, had recently died, which had left a void in both their lives. Jackie was going to surprise her uncle tonight with a visit so as to lift both their spirits.

Dr. Bill Tanner was having a very busy day. As an emergency medicine physician, he was well versed in the stressors of being bombarded with urgent and emergent medical issues. Today was no different than any other day in the emergency department. His niece Jackie had just popped in without notice and he had just encouraged her to wait for a while until he could get a few minutes' break. He had to attend to an unconscious man that was just brought in by the paramedics.

Joe had felt compelled to follow the ambulance to the hospital. He might be able to offer some firsthand information to the treating physician. He spoke with a Dr. Tanner and reported the incident to the doctor. He waited in the waiting room as he wanted to learn the outcome of this unconscious man's fate.

Jackie was also hanging out in the waiting room as she hoped to get to spend a few minutes with her uncle. As she patiently waited, she noticed a man stealing glimpses of her and smiling at her when she looked his way.

As Joe waited to hear the fate of the unconscious man, he looked up and saw the most beautiful woman he had ever seen. He wanted to meet this woman, but attempting to pick up a date in an emergency department waiting room ... well, it just seemed morbid. After throwing around a few quick smiles her way, he noticed that she was also smiling.

Dr. Tanner was doing everything in his power to save the man who had been made unconscious by a traumatic head injury. He was following all the proper protocols as well as utilizing his years of education, wisdom, and experience to save this man's life.

Jackie felt compelled to allow this stranger, the one who was flirting with her, into her life. She gave Joe the opportunity to introduce himself, and the two of them instantaneously hit it off. It would take over seven years, a marital bond, two children, and two pet dogs before they would discover that today was the day Joe paid it forward by paying for Jackie's drink.

Dr. Tanner, out of confidentiality, never shared the unconscious man's fate with Joe. Did Tom live, die, or become crippled for the rest of his life?

This was a fictional story, but it iterates in one way how our actions and reactions connect with those around us, just as a rock thrown in a lake doesn't only affect the impaction spot, but it affects everything that comes in contact with the ripples that the wave generates. Similarly, our daily lives have far-reaching energies. A balance of energy must be restored in one way or another.

Oh, as for Tom, seven years later, he did end up paying it forward, as Dr. Tanner unknowingly received a free drink from him while going through the drive-thru at the coffee shop near his hospital.

HAPPY PLACE

I have a lot of stressors in my life. I'm sure you do, too. We all have matters and situations that add stressors to our daily lives. Of course, a stressor can be a positive motivating factor, but more often than not, the stressors that we encounter end up adding obstacles to our goals. To overcome our stressful situations, we instill several means to combat and overcome them. Needless to say, the best means to diffuse stress is to maintain a balance of mind, body, and spirit. This involves optimizing our health by getting regular exercise, eating a heart-healthy diet, staying well hydrated, and getting adequate and regular amounts of sleep. It also involves spending time with family and friends and connecting with our spiritual being, whether that be by attending church, praying, or meditating. One of the most successful and positive means of dealing with one's stress is to go to your happy place.

Many of you know and agree with that de-stressor method, while some of you are thinking that I have lost my mind. "Really, a happy place? Isn't that for kindergartners?" Sure, a happy place can be for elementary children, but it can also be for high schoolers, college students, businesspeople, priests, and physicians, to name a few groups. In other words, a happy place is a place for everyone.

A happy place is a virtual place inspired by one's imagination. It allows the person to stay or return to a happy state of mind by reducing their stress and allowing them to stay calm in the moment. You are able to go to your happy place at any time, anywhere, and anyplace. Your eyes can be open or closed. The result is an instantaneous calming effect. Come along for the ride as I take you to some of my happy places.

I am sitting on the beach with my family. The sun is high above the sky. The heat from the sun's rays penetrates my skin with just the right amount of warmth. My wife sits next to me as she allows the cool tide water to tickle her toes. The gentle breeze of the wind blows onto my body with the perfect amount to balance out the heat from the sun. The coconut trees behind us sway back and forth. My daughter is in front of me making a sandcastle. I can hear her giggle with wonder as she frolics about the beach. Behind her lies the crystal-clear ocean with dolphins swimming and playing with one another. No one else is on the beach for miles—no one. I am as content and happy as I can be.

I am in a cold sterile room with other adoptive parents. We are in China, the province of Anhui, in the city of Hefei, on a frigid January afternoon. The windows are open, and the wind carries in the briskness of the air. The heat in the room is turned off. We are all trying but failing to wait patiently, then the door opens. Seven women with six crying babies march into the front of the room. The time has come. For the first time, my wife and I come face to face with Feng Chao Ling. Tomorrow, this 14-month-old baby girl will officially become our daughter, Rebecca Ling Pace. But today, we get to hold her for the first time. As the nanny hands this child over to me, I begin to cry, with a joy and love so powerful that I cannot express them in words. My life, my family, is now complete.

I find myself back in my childhood home. It is Christmas morning, 1975. The memory of our Christmas Eve party the night before, with family and friends, still lingers in my mind. But Santa Claus has now come to our home and gone, leaving behind gifts that I hope were on my wish list. I wake up in my room, look at the clock, and see that it is 4:30 a.m. Shoot, I can't wake up my parents yet. What to do, what to do? I try to go back to sleep, but I quickly realize that's not going to happen. I lie in bed trying to recall what I actually put on my wish list. After what seems to be like an eternity, I look at the clock again and it is 6:30 a.m. It is still too early, but I persuade my brother to get up, and we both head out to wake up the folks. I rush to the family room and my dreams are a reality. Santa Claus has left us with toys on top of more toys. This Christmas morning is the best ever.

It is a hot, humid day in August. I am wearing a tuxedo, and the heat and dampness on my body cause the shirt to stick to my skin. I find myself in the middle of Georgia, surrounded by family and friends. My cousin comes into the room and is excited about the vest that came with his tuxedo. The rest of the guys are wearing cummerbunds, as am I. I realize that the vest is mine and the cummerbund is his and I have to wrestle the vest from his body. The time has come. We all get in position, the music starts playing, and I see my beautiful fiancée walk down the aisle escorted by her father. The time has arrived for two to become one. Soon, we say our vows, I kiss my bride, and my best friend has become my wife. Life is good and I am happy.

Remember that the descriptions above are my happy places, not yours. The point is that one's happy place is any situation, any location—anything that makes the visionary happy. Some people would wonder how a frigid room could cause happiness. Wouldn't someone want to optimize the temperature in their virtual world? Perhaps, but for me, the day I adopted my daughter brings me happiness just by thinking about it. Not just when she was placed in my arms but everything and every essence of that time made me happy. The joy of having your happy place is that it is yours and yours alone. The simplicity of having your happy place is that it exists in your mind, on your own terms, at any time. Sometimes, my happy place is a place that doesn't exist in reality, a situation that I anticipate will occur later in my life, or more often, one of my fondest memories.

Try it out sometime. Make your happy place as vivid and real as you want it to be. The ideas are limitless, as your imagination is the pilot to your destination.

Medical Experiences From China

Back in 2018, I visited China with my family, and I was able to experience some medically related stories worth sharing with you. I feel compelled to preface this topic with an explanation. Many Westerners have a preconceived notion that China and other Asian countries practice archaic and non-evidence-based medicine. That being said, both Eastern and Western medicines are practiced in China, and a lot of the Eastern-based therapies are evidence based. The stories I am telling skew the realities of everyday medicine in China, but I am sharing them due to the impact that they had on me.

One member of our tour group forgot her blood pressure medication and she had to seek medical treatment to get a replacement prescription. She was taken to a local private Beijing hospital where she was appropriately treated. She could have chosen to go to a public hospital, but the wait would have been several hours rather than several minutes. She informed me that they placed a hold charge on her credit card for 3,000 RMB (approximately $470) before they would see and treat her. Her experience was pleasant, and she reported the waiting room setting to be luxurious. Her final bill including the medicine was 275 RMB (about

$42). I suspect her experience would have been quite different at a public facility. This does not seem much different from our medical system here in the United States. And yes, she received the same medication that she was prescribed back home.

I had the chance to interview our guide about his views of the Chinese medical system. He informed me that he was overall satisfied with his medical care. He pays a monthly fee for his health insurance, which covers him and his family for about 85-90 percent of the cost. Even so, he has to pay the entire bill up front and then gets reimbursed for the insurance's portion. He just started seeing a primary care physician and reports that this is a new concept that is slowly catching on in China. Previously, many Chinese people only went to the hospital when they were sick, and most do not have a primary physician. He is concerned that the poor are not adequately insured and that they often do not receive the necessary medical treatments that are available. His health insurance unfortunately does not cover all the China provinces. So, if he gets ill and needs medical attention away from his home base of Beijing, he may not be fully insured and would need to pay the bill out of his own pocket. His company does give a six-week maternity leave and a two-week paternity leave. He can choose to transfer his paternity leave time to his wife's maternity leave.

While we were in Chengdu, China's Sichuan province, my wife had the opportunity to get an ear massage. It was quite interesting from my perspective and different from the alternative and dangerous ear candling treatment that we are aware of back in the States. I was skeptical, informing my wife that she may get a perforated tympanic membrane or a scratched auditory canal, but she wanted to proceed with the massage anyway. The ear massage involves the practitioner taking a tuning fork and placing it on the bones near the ear. I suspect this is to allow the massage therapist to determine the amount, thickness, and depth of cerumen in the auditory canal. Perhaps it also allows for the oscillatory effect to loosen the cerumen from the canal wall. Or else this is all a hocus-pocus song and dance. The practitioner then proceeded to place a tissue in my wife's ear, along with a feather-tipped device to remove any cerumen. My wife did not have much cerumen removed, but one of our traveling companions grossed out most of the onlookers as gobs of cerumen and possibly other stuff were removed from his ear canal.

Prior to going to China, I was informed that I might be urinating into a hole. In place of standard Western toilets, the bathrooms of many Eastern countries have an area with a hole covered by a raised rim. Nicknamed "squatty potties" by us Westerners, this method of defecating is more anatomically correct than that offered by our sit-down toilets. Fortunately, I used only one of those toilets to urinate, but aiming was still more of a challenge than I am used to. For those wishing to travel to Asia, unless you are in a rural area, most of the cities now also have Western-style toilets. However, don't forget to take your own toilet paper ... just in case.

While in Yangshuo, a city in China's Guangxi region, I ventured into a medicine shop to peruse the goods. Many of our prescription medications can be purchased over the counter in China. I asked the attendant for penicillin but was informed that they were out of it. The attendant spoke some English, and she proceeded to ask me about my symptoms. I was not ill, but I made up a few symptoms and she suggested amantadine. Amantadine is an antiviral medication used to treat Influenza A and Parkinson's disease. I respectfully declined the prescription. She then asked if I would be willing to take Chinese medicine, to which I responded yes. I received a ten-day supply of some form of cold remedy for under three dollars. In the local pharmacy that I visited, I was able to see both Western and Eastern medicines. When I walked into the pharmacy, the woman was measuring and mixing some kinds of roots. I was informed by our tour guide that most of the people, at least in Beijing, get their medicines distributed from the hospitals rather than the pharmacies.

During our Yangshuo visit, I was also able to participate in a tai chi lesson taught by a local tai chi master. Tai chi is an ancient martial art that is practiced both as a defense mechanism and for its health benefits. It has been shown to alleviate chronic pain and fight stress. Having the Green Lotus Peak with water in the background during the tai chi lesson was both soothing and mesmerizing for my soul.

During a shopping excursion in Guilin, a city in China's Guangxi region, I came across a fish pedicure shop. Several tanks filled with fish were lined up with seats behind the tanks. These fish, garra rufa fish, are utilized for fish pedicures. Customers stick their feet into the tanks, and the fish nibble away at dead, calloused skin. These fish, also known as "doctor fish," are inch-long toothless carp. Though effective, this type of pedicure is not advised as the fish may transmit bacteria to one's skin, causing a serious skin infection. A few years ago, this type of pedicure arrived in the United States, but has since been banned in several states.

My experiences in China were vast. I am fortunate to share a part of these experiences with you. Some people may think these medical-related stories depict Chinese medicine as antiquated and ridiculous. But Chinese medicine has existed for thousands of years, and my allopathic approach to medicine has only been around for hundreds of years. Approaches to medicine are ever evolving. One day, we may all come to the conclusion that a mesh of both perspectives will result in the best outcomes.

THE SANCTITY OF LIFE

Envision a world where your best friend, closest relative, lover, hero, or child vanishes from existence, never to be known to you. That is what happens when a human fetus is aborted from its mother's womb. Your life would forever be changed in ways that you could not even imagine. The late nights chatting, gone; the memory of a vacation, gone; their caressing touch, gone. It is fascinating to me to look at my life in the perspective of what could have been in a manner to appreciate what I have in the present.

Abortion is obviously a hot topic for debate with both sides having their feet deeply dug in the sand, unwilling to budge an inch. I would like you to indulge me and listen to my perspective on life. I believe in the sanctity of life from conception until death. Our society struggles with what constitutes the beginning of a human being's life.

I believe that life starts at the moment the sperm penetrates the egg. From a religious standpoint, I feel that, at that specific moment in time, the human's soul enters into the being. From a medical standpoint, the potential for life has begun with the formation of the zygote, or fertilized ovum. Then there is the argument of when a woman biologically becomes a mother. Again, for me, it is when the potential for life in her body changes into kinetic energy.

Kinetic energy is energy set in motion, and this equates to two gametes forming into a zygote, setting off the kinetic energy to develop into a full living and breathing creature.

It is interesting how some women do not feel any different during the time of conception, whereas others will swear to you that they can pinpoint the exact time of conception. It is also understandable that some people see the human zygote as simply a few cells invading the body, similar to cancer cells. They feel that it is their right to extinguish these cells from their body as if they were cancer cells. But the kinetic energy that is set in motion with cancer cells and with fetal cells results in two very different outcomes. It is very easy for someone to end an activity before their kinetic energy reaches its full potential, and that goes the same for human fetal cells.

Women will abort human fetal cells for various reasons. They will do so for personal rights, personal freedoms, incest, rape, coercions, or medical reasons. I am not going to place judgment on them by any means. Right or wrong, they will have to live with their decision. I contend that the only ethical and moral abortion is when the women's life is in imminent danger. Again, I'm not passing judgment on anyone, as that is my ethical standard and another's may not mesh with mine. However, I would just ask that a woman hear the following messages before deciding to abort their fetus.

As a medical physician, I have dealt with many women who have had abortions. What I have found is that the majority of these women have emotional issues later in life, and many of them are on antidepressants. Some have confided in me that they feel so much guilt for aborting their child. Others have chronic pain and suffering because they cannot come to grips or forgive themselves of their past actions. I rarely came across a woman who regretted birthing their child. I have had teenage mothers, previously headed down a life of frustration and insecurities, who have said that their child was the best thing that ever happened to them. I have cared for children and adults with Down syndrome who have brought love and joy to me, their families, and frankly everyone they meet.

I certainly understand why a young woman would want to flush out cells that are going to change her life forever, whether it be for career matters, financial matters, or otherwise. But these women seem to look only at the fears of being a mother. Studies have shown that when a mother is able to visually see their fetal child on an ultrasound, their whole perspective on their future changes, and many of them opt to proceed with birthing their child rather than getting an abortion. To me, using abortion as a form of birth control is like wanting a horse disqualified because you didn't like the way the race started. Rape and incest are particularly touchy matters, but the woman still has a part of her in that child. If she is unable to care for that child, which is understandable, then adoption is a viable option. However, conception due to rape and incest, for many, equates to a disqualified horse race.

I heard someone tell a parable once that God gave the cure for cancer to humankind, but the humans aborted the fetus who was to make the discovery. On the flip side, one could make the argument that we aborted another Hitler. That being said, we adopted our daughter from China. She is now a beautiful, intelligent, caring, and loving young teenage woman, and her future looks bright. She has brought so much joy to me and my wife, her grandparents, family, and friends. She has influenced the world in her own writings, drawings, and photos. This world is a better place with her in it. I am so blessed and grateful that my daughter's biological mother had the courage and fortitude to see her pregnancy to the end, despite the risks she endured living in a socialist country. Had my daughter been aborted, the world would have lost a good soul, and my family's lives would look so different today.

You know when you throw a rock into the water, a splash occurs, and then a ripple takes effect. From that one action, several other actions are set in motion. Everything around the ripple is affected in some way, good or bad. The same thing occurs with our actions, and determining to have an abortion or seeing the pregnancy to the end is like throwing a boulder into the pond. Any woman contemplating an abortion has a very difficult decision to make, and I pray every day that life becomes that ripple in the water.

So, now let's look at another hot topic on life, one's view on capital punishment. While one political view has decided that abortion is a woman's right, they contend that ending an adult's life is not a human right at all. Whereas, the polar political view sees abortion as inherently wrong but feels humans have the right to end an adult's life at the discretion of the courts. I hold that the sanctity of life is sacred and that the only acceptable means to end another's life is when one's own life is in imminent danger.

I will be the first one to tell you that if a family member or friend were viciously and violently murdered by someone, emotionally I would want to end the murderer's life. I would be filled with so much anger and rage that I would need to seek psychological treatment to settle down my feelings. As cooler thoughts prevail, I could not live with myself knowing that I decided to combat murder with murder.

Capital punishment is when the courts authorize the legal killing of an individual as a criminal punishment. The legal system or families of the victims will look to this as a means for justice. Good and reasonable arguments for this method point out that justice has been served, and the murderer has been eliminated, never to inflict injury or death on other individuals. Also, society does not have to pay hundreds of thousands of dollars caring for the criminal. They will cite the fact that other countries with strict capital punishment laws have low murder rates. These are all reasonable decisions, but I believe that life and death should only be at the hand of God.

While I believe that criminals' lives should not be eradicated by the courts, I do believe that criminals that meet the requirements for capital punishment need to pay for their crime. These individuals should be locked up in a prison for the rest of their days on Earth. Though this is an expensive task, I feel that it is a societal obligation. We would need to be humane in our handling of those incarcerated. Unfortunately, our prison system seems to take this to an extreme, giving the criminals certain luxuries that not even the victim's families can afford.

The question that gets raised is whether or not the murderer is able to be rehabilitated. Frankly, and understandably, most families of the victims don't care if the murderer can be rehabilitated or not. In my opinion, the answer to this question is necessary, not so much because we want them to be allowed back into society, but more so for them to make amends for their actions. Life is precious, and if a murderer can work to right their wrong, though some believe that can never be done, we, as a society, owe that to the murderer's victim.

For some crimes, the decision of guilt is obvious, but for other cases, the conclusion is based on ambiguous or faulty evidence. The concern that everyone has with capital punishment cases is that we might kill an innocent person. Cases have existed where DNA evidence has exonerated the imprisoned while these individuals were on death row. The anguish and misery an incarcerated innocent person endures are evil and inhumane. Once capital punishment is enacted, it cannot be reversed. Yet some will say that these individuals are the collateral damage that occurs in order to capture the guilty. That may be their view until they become the collateral damage themselves.

I'm sure that after reading on these topics of abortion and capital punishment, emotions have been stirred and feelings are spiking. Needless to say, I suspect that society will be wrestling with these matters of life and death well after I leave this world. By interacting and having a respectful dialogue with all sides, we may one day come to a decision that our society as a whole can live with.

A PUGILISTIC BOND

My dad was a hardworking, ethically driven family man. Having been dealt some unfortunate cards and equipped with only a ninth-grade formal education, my dad built a successful auto parts business. Though he loathed his daily job, he loved our family, and he demonstrated this love through his actions.

I was a young teenage boy, and, like most teenagers, I thought the world revolved around me. At the time, I was in eighth grade and was an average student. I was engrossed in the world of sports. I was on the soccer, basketball, and baseball teams for my elementary school. When I wasn't in school, I was either playing or watching sports.

My father despised most sports. Yet, he would still take the time to drag himself to some of my games. His idea of excitement was getting his hands dirty and tinkering with the engine of his car. My twin brother also shared this idea of fun, and they both were able to develop a strong bond based around this feeling they shared.

Other than the natural bond a child has for a loving and caring parent, I did share one element with my dad. On weekend nights, we would sit in front of the television and watch one of the boxing matches that was highlighted for the evening. We both loved boxing. Sometimes to make the match more engaging, we would bet fifty cents or even an entire dollar on the match. My dad would always let me pick my favorite boxer, and he would sometimes grudgingly take the opponent, understanding the odds were not in his favor. Once the fight was over, we would go back to our daily grind and seem to be worlds apart. However, one night in the fall of 1978, that routine would change forever.

It was a crisp cool fall school night and my dad had just come home after an especially exhausting day at work. As he rushed into the front door, he motioned for me. He told me to change into my exercise clothes and gym shoes so he could show me a surprise. Confused, but excited, I did as he told me, and the next thing I knew we were driving into the inner part of our city.

The sun had set, and my dad eventually parked the car. Up above my head, the building we were about to enter had a blue-and-white neon sign shining brightly in the moonlit sky. The sign illuminated the words *South Broadway Athletic Club*. Still confused, but filled with anticipation, I had no idea why we were there. The wooden steps creaked underneath our feet as we walked to the second floor. I could hear voices talking and shouting in the distance above us. I was hearing familiar sounds, and I thought to myself, "Is this for real or am I living in a dreamworld?"

When we finally reached the top of the stairs, the opening expanded into a large room. In one corner of the room, people were jumping ropes. In another corner, small inflated leather bags hung from a platform and a rhythmic cadence of beats emanated from them as they were being punched. On one side, young men and women, with their hands wrapped in cloth, were punching into the air, while on the other side, similar athletic types were smacking around large tubular structures that were hanging from the ceiling. And there it was, in the center of the room, shining so brightly, I looked in awe as if I had found the Holy Grail. There, in the center of the room, sat an official-sized boxing ring. The icing on the cake were the two pugilists sparring about in the ring.

My dad looked over at me, let me know that he discovered this place, and asked if I wanted to try my hand at boxing. I thought to myself, "Are you kidding me? Do birds fly?" My dad was telling me that this could be our thing together, but the choice was mine, and mine alone, to make. With a resounding yes, I spent the next two hours learning the very basics of boxing. Over time, I learned that to be a successful boxer, you should not close your eyes or rotate your neck when you see the punch coming.

For the next three years, my dad would drive me to my boxing practices and matches. I was actually a very good boxer. I won't brag and tell you my record, but I will say that I was a contender you would most likely place your bet on. I learned that I was a natural counterpuncher. A boxing counterpuncher is someone who patiently waits for their opponent to make a mistake and then capitalizes on that mistake with an uppercut to the chin or a hook to the jaw.

My boxing years were not really about the exercise I received with the sport but more about the relationship I developed with my father and the lessons I learned from such a disciplined sport. Some people may wonder how I could participate in such a seemingly barbaric sport. Perhaps they have a valid opinion, but I would not have changed my boxing days for the world.

Several months after I started boxing, I was entering high school. You only get one first impression, and my introduction to my fellow freshman classmates as a boxer had far-reaching advantages. My popularity soared in a private all-boys Catholic school set outside the city, where I was probably the first boxer that any of them had ever met. This popularity would have consequences, though, as one classmate felt that I was taking away too much of the attention. He challenged me to a fight, brought in a couple pairs of boxing gloves, and we met in the locker room of our school. Surrounded by a large portion of our class, I backed down, stating that the fight would not be fair, and that I could really harm him. Realizing that he was not going to let this go, the fight took place, I knocked him down, and he rose without adverse effects, but with a new respect for me and my sport.

I convinced my grandmother to come see what all the fuss was about as well as see what her son and grandson were bonding over. One day, she finally came to one of my matches. As she sat up in the bleachers, I bounced around the ring with such vigor and determination to show my grandma how good I was at my chosen sport. I was probably too confident at that moment, and the mistake I made cost me an intact nose. My opponent hit my face with just the right angle, my nose shattered, and blood gushed all over my white T-shirt. After the hemorrhage was under control, I walked over to my grandmother with my blood-stained shirt and said, "Well, what did you think—fun, huh?" With disbelief and a look of terror, that was the last boxing match she attended.

Three years into my amateur boxing career, I was practicing for a life-changing boxing match, when my coach and I made a grave mistake. We forgot to put Vaseline on my and my opponent's face. Petroleum jelly is used to minimize the friction that the glove has on the skin, thereby decreasing the likelihood that the skin will tear. A few minutes into the sparring match, our cheeks were cut and our eyes were swollen and closed shut. I would heal over time, but somehow I had to hide this catastrophe from my mother. My mom knew that I was going to the boxing gym, but my dad and I had her believe that I was only punching on the bags, shadow-boxing, and jumping rope.

For the next week, I attempted to avoid my mother face to face. But one night I slipped, and she noticed that my left eye was swollen and partially closed. She suddenly realized what I was doing in the boxing gym. I tried to convince her that the heavy bag swung back and hit me in the eye, but she wouldn't latch on to that lie. Appearing angry, she shouted, "You want to fight, I'll show you how to fight." She then took some swipes to my backside, and then ran out of the room crying. My dad then walked in, informed me that my boxing days were over, and reminded me not to let my mom know that he signed the release forms giving his permission for me to box.

I'm not going to argue with anyone about the benefits or hazards of the sport of boxing. I am well aware of the inherent dangers in a sport where the goal is to disable your opponent. I have arthritis in my hands and neck as a result of the sport, and I am at an increased risk of developing dementia in my later years. However, I would not have changed my time boxing for anything in this world. The lessons I learned were far reaching and everlasting. I was taught the importance of self-discipline, delayed gratification, commitment, passion, perseverance, and preparation.

But more importantly, the sport allowed me and my dad to lessen our gap and create a stronger bond. My dad is gone now, but I will see him again once my final bell rings.

DATING

Dating is a rite of passage that most teenagers endure as they mature into adulthood. The social interaction of two individuals with the intent to become romantically involved with one another can be a daunting task. Planning to ask someone out on a date can be exhilarating, frustrating, frightening, and uplifting all at once. I have been on several first dates in my life. Some have been fun, others disappointing, but I learned something about myself with each one. Here are my stories.

One of my first dating experiences was one not born out of love but with much infatuation. I had put this girl on a pedestal and yearned to be her boyfriend. I was on a high when she agreed to go out with me. Before going out on our date, I had to come inside and meet her mother. I had a purity about myself and held my virginity as a sacred bond to be given up only to my future wife. I was naturally shocked when this woman took me aside, told me to have a good time, and make damn sure that I didn't get her daughter pregnant. Whoa! The only thing I was looking for was a hug and maybe a kiss. Needless to say, our relationship did not pass the test of time, and she broke up with me a few months later.

One of her classmates took a liking to me. She was cute and we seemed to hit it off, so I asked her out on a date. I didn't want to blow anything, so I took things slowly and ended our date with a simple goodbye. A few days later, the gossip got back to me that she was so disappointed that I didn't kiss her goodnight, especially when I had kissed her classmate goodnight on our date. Due to her immaturity, she became obsessed with me, and I probably left a possibly good relationship behind. I never did kiss her.

Keep in mind that back in my youth there were no real accessible practical books on dating. Sure, the girls had *Cosmopolitan* for information and guidance, but us guys just had each other. So, you can guess how much false information was passed around. I did learn that if the date went well, it would be OK to ask for a goodnight kiss.

Sometimes I would be put on a blind date. One weekend night in my high school years, my friend set me up with this beautiful blonde girl. She was a fellow Catholic, planned on attending college, was cultured, and even played the piano. We both hit it off immediately, and the night was going well. Then disaster struck and as she came out of the bathroom with one of her friends (we were all together at a high school dance), I noticed that her breath reeked of cigarette smoke. Smoking was a big turnoff for me and a deal breaker, so I had decided that this would be our first and last date. Though it was in her best interest to quit smoking, it was not for me to try to change her bad habits so that we would be a better fit. So I didn't say anything.

When I dropped her off at her home and walked her up to her front door, I reached out my hand to shake hers and say goodnight. Looking startled, she asked if I was going to give her a kiss goodnight. Not wanting to kiss an ashtray, I made the excuse that I had a cold and didn't want to get her sick. She didn't buy that reason and ran into her home crying, running into her mom's arms. I booked out of there quickly so as not to feel the wrath of an upset parent.

Then there was the time I was in the gym working out with weights. I needed a spot while I was bench-pressing, and so I asked this guy to assist me. He was welcoming and for the rest of the workout, we spotted each other when it was needed. Conversing with this guy, we both noticed that we had some similar interests. I was finishing up my workout, when he asked me if maybe we wanted to hang out sometime and get a drink. I said sure and we exchanged numbers. The gym owner told me that he didn't realize I was a gay man. Wait, what? My innocent youth obscured the truth of the matter. I did learn that I was on the receiving end of scheduling a romantic date with this spotter. I had to put my tail between my legs and let him know that I was a straight man, and so that first date never happened.

Though that date never happened, one date I was on turned out to not even be a date. When I was in college, I was involved in the school's music extracurricular program. I became good friends with one of the other participants. She had asked me to come over and said she would cook dinner. We had a fabulous time that evening, and I was excited about the prospect of our future. As I left her apartment, she walked me to the door. I decided I should say goodnight with a kiss. As I pulled back after kissing her, I noticed that she had that deer-in-the-headlights expression, and I realized that I had grossly misjudged the entire evening. Though we stayed friends, the atmosphere was much different after that night.

I have been on several first dates in my life. To describe these dates by using only one word, I would say that these dates have been either obnoxious, polar, encouraging, frightening, disturbing, weird, or exciting. But my last first date was the best as it was the one where I met my wife.

After medical school, while in my residency, I didn't have much time to do anything but engage in medicine. I had moved to Savannah, Georgia, and I didn't have any friends in the area. As an avid scuba diver at that time, I started searching for dive partners. I used the now-defunct America Online Instant Messaging (AOL IM) program to find and chat with other divers. I quickly discovered that this method was a great way to meet others to, well, perhaps date. It seemed a little creepy, but the nurses at the hospital wouldn't go out with me, so I felt compelled to use any tool available. These days, dating apps are in vogue, and my AOL IM use may have paved the way for their success.

So, after chatting with this woman (I hoped and guessed she was female) on AOL, we progressed our relationship to telephone calls. This person certainly sounded like a female, with a teacher voice and heavy Southern accent. Finally, we met at Garfield's Restaurant for a face-to-face date. This beautiful woman was a Baptist Southern belle and I was an Italian Yankee Catholic. We didn't seem like a good fit initially, but twenty-two years later and we are still happily married. Thanks, AOL; you helped me meet my best friend.

My dating days are over, but as the years quickly pass, I will live somewhat vicariously through my daughter's eyes, as she will be at a dating age soon. But my vantage point will be from an entirely different perspective, as her father. So, young men, bring your A-game on, with respect and admiration, for my daughter's hand.

WHY MEDICINE?

I, like many of my colleagues, have been posed with the question, "Why did you go into the medical field?" This is usually followed by "If you had to do it all over again, would you still be a doctor?" As physicians, we make a wonderful living, yet we also have one of the highest suicide rates of any profession. When you factor in all of the school debt incurred, the many years of training, the daily stressors we endure, along with literally making life-and-death decisions, anyone would be skeptical of entering our profession. If making money is the main factor in one's decision, there are plenty of professions that have higher salaries than us, when all factors are taken into consideration. That being said, no one should ever go into medicine with their main goal to make a lot of money. They will eventually get burned out, and they will likely ultimately do a disservice to their patients.

So, why did I go into the medical field? When I was in high school, I excelled in and thoroughly enjoyed the math and science subjects. By my junior year, I knew that I was destined to migrate toward the sciences, but I still had no idea of my chosen profession; medicine wasn't even on the radar. But my three-week social service project would alter the trajectory of my search. I was assigned as a nurse's aide at Cardinal Glennon Children's Hospital. I did all the scut-work that my nurse assigned to me. But with that experience, I fell in love with the thought of helping those in need. I met with doctors who took the time to talk to me, and this allowed me to realize that medicine was the perfect choice for my profession. I would be able to intertwine the scientific aspect of critical thinking and puzzle-like solutions with the social aspect of human interaction. Furthermore, family medicine has allowed me to analyze and treat the gestalt of the human being.

Medicine, like most if not all of the various health professions, allows the professional to fulfill a human need. Most of us yearn to help others in need. We are driven with the understanding that our talents, expertise, and love for our fellow beings help make this world a better place. We find ourselves in situations that some people cannot fathom. Just look at how health professionals, among other professions, stepped up to the plate and delivered care during the great coronavirus pandemic. We yearn to see our fellow humans heal from their ailments.

During college, I majored in biology and took all the pre-medical courses, and I was planning to go to medical school. But as I was approaching graduation, I became skeptical of my decision. College allowed me to be exposed to many other available career choices, and I became somewhat confused. Being a pre-med student made me a magnet for getting dates. The brothers at my Catholic school reminded me that gathering money shouldn't be the main factor in life. Furthermore, they instilled in me values that were copacetic with my faith.

By graduation, I was confused on what to do, as my desire to become a physician was muddied by my motivating factors. Was I still wanting to enter the medical field based on my love for science and human beings? Was I more motivated by the attention I was getting and the money I would make? I certainly wanted to be comfortable and financially secure in life, but I couldn't make money the focus. So, at graduation, I took a break from my plans of becoming a doctor.

I spent the next three years as a research assistant at Washington University in St. Louis. I enjoyed working daily with test tubes and DNA at my lab station. This solidified my respect for and knowledge of the basic sciences and kept me on a scientific pathway. I entered graduate school with the intention to become an exercise physiologist. As I started taking my first-year graduate coursework, my classmates and I were scattered about with all the first-year medical students who were taking the same courses. The only course that we didn't share was gross anatomy, as that was reserved for the medical students.

By the middle of the school year, after interacting with the medical students, I yearned to change my direction to becoming a physician. I dropped out of graduate school after the first year, spent the next year preparing for medical school, worked as a lab assistant starting up a molecular genetics lab, and entered medical school the following year.

I was on a high when I received my acceptance letter for the class of 1996 at the University of Missouri-Columbia School of Medicine. That day I felt that I had arrived, only to later discover that this was just the beginning. Medical school was one of the most difficult endeavors I have endured. The vast amount of information thrown to us was mind boggling. I completed a semester-long statistics course in one week. I received as much information in one day of medical school as I had in over a month of college. After a month of medical school studies, I thought to myself, what have I done? I even wondered if I had made a big mistake, similar to the main character in the movie, *Gross Anatomy*. Eventually, I came to grips with my reality, attacked my studies head on, and finished the arduous and stressful task. I graduated in 1996 with my medical degree.

I was back on a high and mistakenly thought I had arrived again only to realize that I now had residency in front of me. After completing the difficult task of graduating from medical school, I couldn't conceptualize what I was headed into with being an intern. Fortunately, residency programs these days are more humane, but I was one of the unfortunate ones. My family medicine residency program was the most demanding and difficult time of my life. The surgery residents had it even more difficult, and the only relief I had going was the fact that at least I wasn't them.

I recall my beeper pager going off on my first night of call. It was the nurse in the ICU, and she was asking for a Tylenol order for her patient. I was flabbergasted with this request. All my years of medical school knowledge raced through my mind. Could this patient have Tylenol? Would I throw him into acute liver failure? Was he allergic to it? I first told her that maybe she should call the patient's doctor, only for her to remind me that I was the patient's doctor. Oh, yeah! That didn't work, so what to do, what to do? Overwhelmed with what seemed to be a difficult decision, I chose to tap in on the expertise right in front of me. As an ICU nurse, she was taking care of the patient intimately, so I asked what she would do. She informed me that it would be fine to give this patient Tylenol. I learned quickly that while I was making the medical decisions, the inpatient nurses had a deeper connection with their patients, and we were a team of medical professionals caring together for the health and well-being of our patients.

In the middle of my first year in residency, I was burnt out in my chosen field. I was exhausted and overwhelmed, and I had fallen into a deep depression. As new physicians, we were still on a steep logarithmic learning curve, and our mistakes sometimes would be disastrous. I was angry at myself for getting myself into this predicament, and I yearned to have a job cutting grass. With guidance, I found that I was not alone, and I was given the assistance and support to get me through this difficult time. Unfortunately, some of my colleagues were unable to see the light at the end of the tunnel. I heard that one of my associates in a different program across the country succumbed to the darkness and took his own life. I made sure that was not going to happen to me.

By 1999, I had successfully completed my family medical residency program and passed my boards, and I was finally a board-certified family physician. I am fine-tuning and perfecting my chosen profession daily. I am continuously reading medical journals to stay proficient and up to date with medical knowledge. I have now been in the medical field for over twenty-five years. I have learned from my mistakes and grown as a physician in knowledge and wisdom. I am also learning to understand my fellow humans better. I have come to appreciate my patients for who they are, what they want out of life, and not what I want them to be.

Now to answer the question of, if I had it all over again, would I still become a physician? The simple answer is a resounding "Yes!" Certainly, there were times in my medical career when I seriously considered leaving the field, but medicine is my calling, my destiny. Sure, I have had many financial rewards with the salary of a physician, and I am very grateful for that sidebar. However, the true reward is in knowing that I have helped save lives, assisted those in need, and done what my brothers back in college asked me to do, to be of service to my fellow man.

SPORTS AND SPORTING EVENTS

There are those who are totally absorbed in the world of sports, whereas others absolutely loathe the sound of the word. A lot of us are in between loving some sports and not being able to care less for others. Of course, as with anything in life, moderation is key to a balanced life. Let's take a look at why sports are so much a part of our culture. I hope to convince you that sports participation is an important piece in the development of a child or adolescent.

Growing up in St. Louis, I was an avid fan and participant in multiple sporting events. During grade school, I played soccer in the fall, basketball in the winter, and baseball in the spring. Whenever given the opportunity, I found myself sitting in the bleachers watching baseball, peering around a beam watching hockey, or sitting on cold, hard seats watching football. I have fond memories of cheering on my baseball Cardinals, chilling out at the arena celebrating a Blues hockey goal, and walking around with my friends at Busch Stadium.

Some people, however, see no value in sports. They are disgusted at the outrageous salaries that professional athletes make. They are disturbed by the skewed direction of school funding to sporting activities over the arts. Some have horrible memories from their childhood participating in sports. Others simply don't understand the games, as the rules can be complicated. This group may feel that people take sports too seriously. They get upset that our culture is inundated with sporting advertisements and that they have no way to completely avoid them. All of these points are valid and need to be taken into consideration in our society. I could write pages and pages on the negative effects of sports, but my focus with this section is to discuss the positive aspects of sports in our lives.

By sitting in the stands or watching television and cheering on a favorite team, the fans are connecting with one another. Rather than feeling alone in the world, the fan is able to connect with a wider group of like individuals. The team's win becomes their win. They have a sense of belonging with their school, church, city, or organization. Some can connect with previous enemies who share the love of the same team. Being an alumnus of St. John Vianney High School, I still felt connected to my school when I cheered them on to win their first state football championship.

Sports fans are able to escape from their everyday activities. The daily grinds of life with the pressures of school or work create a need to find a release. By watching a sporting event, the fan can focus on the sport and for a short time take a reprieve and forget about the worries of the day. I was able to escape the challenges of being a high school freshman for a few hours as I watched the 1980 "Miracle on Ice" USA Olympic hockey team beat the Russians for the gold medal.

Sports fans can express themselves emotionally for a defined period of time. They can cheer and smile when their team scores a goal, balk at an umpire's decision, and show sadness during a loss. They can dress up in the team's colors or jerseys. Sports fans undergo a roller coaster of emotions, but they understand and know that they can get off the ride at any time. The St. Louis Cardinals' eleventh World Series win was one of my most memorable roller coasters of a ride.

Sports fans can bond with their children. They can watch their children develop and mature, accept defeat, and learn how to appreciate a win. My father did not particularly like sports but we both shared and developed a stronger bond over the sport of boxing.

Sports fans would be able to list numerous other reasons they love sports. The ones above are the most common reasons. Now, let's direct our attention to the athlete. I would like to focus on the amateur run-of-the-mill athlete and not on the Olympic-caliber or professional athlete.

Sports participation has many beneficial aspects for the young athlete and adult. The most obvious one is that by participating in sports, one is able to get physical activity. It is advised that children and youth get at least one hour of moderate to vigorous activity per day. Adults are advised to get at least one hundred and fifty minutes of moderate aerobic activity, seventy-five minutes of vigorous aerobic activity, or a combination of both per week. Most sporting activities fulfill these recommendations, be they individual or group sports. Studies show that adults are more likely to be regular exercisers if they participated in sports in their youth. Some sports like tennis or swimming can persist into adulthood and be a wonderful and lifelong means of exercise.

Sports participation allows the young athlete to develop a strong sense of self-worth. Young athletes can develop higher self-esteem, develop lifelong friendships, learn self-control, and gain a better respect for rules and leaders. Athletes can advance their motor and coordination skills. Sports participation allows the individual to take on challenges and work to overcome them. The young athlete is able to appreciate the value of overcoming obstacles by practicing often in order to perfect his or her goal. They can see the value in striving to reach a goal, and this can carry over into the classroom. They come to understand what a common goal means to the group, and they are more likely to become a team player in the course of their life. This will allow them to develop their communication and problem-solving skills. Sportsmanship is taught through sports, thereby allowing athletes to conduct themselves in a fair and gracious manner. Athletes can learn how to be better followers and how to become leaders.

I have wonderful memories of both my participation in and observance of sporting activities. I am able to divert my attention for a short time to cheer on my favorite team. I am able to bike and swim on a regular basis to maintain my health. I believe that an individual should be open to the concept of sports participation.

These are just a few reasons I believe that children, adolescents, and even adults should participate in sporting activities. I could list many more reasons, but the idea is still the same. Sports participation could be as small as participating in a physical education class. The bottom line is, I believe there is a practically perfect sport for everyone.

The Journey of Traveling

I have a love-hate relationship with traveling. I hate the cost, but I love the research, preparation, journey, hotel stays, restaurant dining, culture, and sightseeing. So the scale is weighted in the favor of traveling. Granted, many people can't afford the exorbitant financial burdens, but there are ways to minimize costs. If a parent cannot afford to travel with their family, when their child gets older, they can send their offspring on a cultural adventure with the assistance of school classes and programs. Let's see why traveling should be an important aspect in your life, even if it takes you out of your comfort zone.

You know the axiom, "It's not the destination, it's the journey"? Have you ever sat down and decided on a travel destination? Choosing the location, the start of the process, is as exciting for me as the final destination. Back when I was younger, it was a thrill to head over to the travel agency and peruse all the travel pamphlets. These days, I sit in the comfort of my home and do my research by surfing the web. Of course, a travel agent still gives the added benefit that you may not want to pass up.

Once a destination is selected, the next step of the journey is the preparation phase. For me, this is the most exciting point of the journey. I go back on the internet and continue reviewing local sites, hotels, museums, restaurants, and activities my family and I would enjoy. Then I absorb myself in reading about the local area's history and culture. This part of the journey can take weeks. I also believe it is the most important part of my travel journey. This immersion will allow the traveler to better appreciate and get much more out of the chosen destination.

After the preparation stage is complete, it is time to actually head to the destination. Packing my suitcase, completing my to-do lists, and finally heading out the door is a process that seems similar to the pilot's pre-flight checklist before takeoff. I have downloaded packing travel apps on my smartphone that have done most of the organizational work for me. Now that the car is packed, the time has come, and I will soon be on my way.

Several modes of transportation are available to reach my destination. I have traveled by vehicle, airplane, train, and ship. Two travel options I have yet to have the opportunity to partake in are the motor home option and the much longer method of walking or biking. Each one has advantages and disadvantages, and any mode may be selected based on convenience, time, cost, or personal preference.

So, the day has come, and you are on your way to your chosen destination. Let's delve into the wonderful experiences that you will enjoy on your journey. Below, I have listed a generalized synopsis of my most favorable memories with my forms of transportation.

AUTOMOBILE

- Ability to leave on one's own time
- Listening to the radio, playing car games with the family, and having deep, intimate family conversations
- Stopping along the route to see places and sites of interest

AIRPLANE

- Sitting in the airport terminal reading a book, eating at a new restaurant, and checking out the shops
- Flying high above the clouds, looking out the window, and daydreaming about God's beautiful creation
- Getting to the travel destination quickly

TRAIN

- Having luggage nearby, accessible, and ready to pick up immediately upon arrival
- The gentle rocking motion of the train as it rolls down the tracks
- Reading a book and then looking out the window and watching the scenery whisk by

SHIP

- Having multiple onboard activities easily accessible and readily available
- Being able to stop at multiple ports of entry
- Being only a few steps away from the room

I understand that disadvantages exist with each form of travel, and some people may focus on these negative aspects, thereby blunting their travel experience. I certainly have had challenging traveling times where everything seemed to have gone wrong. However, I still managed to pull a memorable experience out of each one. The nice thing about our memories is that we tend to forget the bad and remember the good. Even with some memories that seemed disastrous at the time, once we look back on them we might even chuckle or smile.

Your journey continues once you arrive at your destination. Here, I list a general overview of the pleasures I have received from my traveling experiences:

ACCOMMODATIONS

- Viewing a city from the balcony of a luxurious high-rise hotel
- Having a nice compact room on a ship
- Deciding to eat in with the assistance of room service
- Living among the locals in a hostel setting
- Experiencing nature up close in a tent
- Sheltering in a cabin on a cold winter day

SIGHTSEEING

- Marveling at the ornate and unique architectural wonders of the buildings
- Being absorbed in the cultural diversity of the local people and history of the area
- Feeling a sense of awe from the visual beauty of the landscape

- Visiting a specific place that was previously researched in the preparation phase
- Experiencing local sights that either are man-made or were created by God
- Going geocaching in the area, seeing new sites along the way, and capturing the memory with a photo

Shopping and Dining

- Popping in and out of eclectic stores and souvenir shops
- Having a beignet for breakfast at an outdoor cafe
- Finding that perfect memento to place on a shelf at home
- Eating delicious local cuisine for lunch
- Contributing to the local commerce
- Relaxing over dinner while watching the sunset

Personal Enrichment

- Stress reliever from daily workload and preventing work burnout
- Increased level of confidence and creative process
- Handling adversity and uncertainty more reliably and confidently
- Being in a better mood, boosting happiness, and reducing stress
- Gaining a real-world education
- Bonding and developing relationships with others, thereby bringing the world closer together

As my time comes to a close in my chosen destination and I am getting ready to head home, I close my eyes and mentally review all of the opportunities I experienced on my journey. I also capture the moments, either in my writing or in photographs. I like to have them in order to review the events in the future.

Traveling will widen your horizons and enrich your life in ways that cannot be done by always staying home. Traveling will help bring our world together, and it will also unify us as human beings. Traveling will allow memories to be shared with friends and family. Traveling will help show us that the true value is not in the destination, but in the journey. Now, go pack your bags.

TOILET PAPER ROLLS AND OTHER BATHROOM STUFF

When you hang a roll of toilet paper on the dispenser, do you put it so the paper hangs over or under the roll? In my opinion, this says a lot about the person. Scientific studies suggest that over-hangers are more assertive individuals, whereas under-hangers seem to be the submissive type. I tend to agree with that because I believe this task of hanging toilet paper really tells a lot about a person. The over-hangers are confident, driven individuals who thrive on law and order. The under-hangers have an artistic flair about them, throwing caution to the wind as they frolic about with their days. Being an over-hanger myself, I get flustered when I find our toilet paper rolls at home have been placed in the under position. Yes, I feel compelled and often change the roll into the over-hang position.

My wife, who apparently oscillates between being dominant and submissive, has put the roll on in both directions. What does that say about her? I guess, without upsetting the feminists out there, she is saying, "I'm a woman, hear me roar" as she is going to do what she is going to do. Don't even get me started on my daughter. I don't know which way she places the toilet paper roll, probably because as a typical teenager, she won't allow me in her bathroom.

Speaking of changing the toilet paper roll, how long do you wait until you change the toilet paper roll? Now, I am one to admit that, for some reason, I don't like replacing the roll. When I see that the roll is coming to an end, I start rationing the paper so that I am able to leave at least one or two sheets on the roll covering up the roller. Yeah, that's a doomsday situation for the next user, but heaven forbid I pull off the last sheet; then I feel obligated to replace the roll. I know that as you are reading this, you are thinking, "What a bastard," but let's face it, many of you do the same thing. If I am misguided on this subject, then someone let me know and I will go and seek counseling.

Still in the bathroom, or, as my European friends like to say, the water closet room, one has to decide if they are going to keep the toilet seat up or down. You would think the answer to this one is simple, but it's more complicated than just believing that men often leave the seat up and women always keep it down. While I suspect it is true that women always keep the seat down, that's not the case for men, or at least this man. When I have to go and relieve my bodily fluids, I have the daunting task of deciding to touch the toilet seat. If it is already up, I'm good to go, but often that's not the case. The deciding factor in my case is based on my location.

If I am at home, sometimes I leave the toilet seat up and sometimes down, depending on my mood. I just make sure that I clean it for the comfort of my wife, daughter, and guests. However, when I leave the room, I make sure that both the toilet seat and cover are in the down position. I don't want to hear a splash as someone's buttocks get stuck in the bowl. I keep the cover down as it is more aesthetically pleasing in the home. Also, I used to have cats and I was always fearful that they would slip in and drown, or worse, use it as their playpen. If I am at work, I leave it up if it is dirty. I'm not about to clean it, and I certainly don't want to be blamed for making it dirty. If I am in a public restroom, well, let's just say I do what I can. No, you won't catch gonorrhea from a toilet set, but other diseases are certainly lurking around, and I don't want any of that.

When I go into a public washroom—yeah, that's my fancy way of saying bathroom or restroom—I have to figure out how to safely leave the facility. Why am I in danger, you say? With all those microscopic organisms hiding about, the last thing I want is to take one with me. Studies have shown that up to a third of people don't wash their hands after using the toilet. When these people exit the room, they touch the door with their dirty, grubby, disease-infected hands. So, now, how am I supposed to get safely out of the room?

I'm ecstatic when I see that the public washroom is doorless. This allows me to get in and out safely. Some doors have that hands-free foot door opener while others are swing doors. These doors I also welcome with open arms. It's the door handle that presents a problem. When I come across one of those, I get some paper towels and exit. But one time I found myself in a predicament. I was finishing up washing my hands, when this guy came out from the toilet stall, skipped the sink, and opened the door with his nasty hands. I tried to abort my wash and escape before the door closed, but to no avail. Looking for a way out of my unfortunate situation, no paper towels were available, as only hand dryers were installed on the walls, and the bozo had used all the toilet paper. Feeling nauseous, I took the plunge, turned the door handle, and left the room. I immediately went to another washroom to wash my hands. The moral of this story, and my public service announcement, is, "Wash your damn hands, people."

So for the third of you who don't wash your hands, I realize that you don't think those digits of yours are dirty. If, for some reason, you are that special gift from God who is 100 percent pure, good for you. But wash your hands anyway. Don't get me started on the filth on your cellphone.

Keep in mind, most of the information I shared with you is from personal experiences and wisdom, so don't be quoting this information to your friends when you are trying to win an argument. And kids, certainly don't be referencing this in your term papers. That being said, as you go through life, you'll agree that I am spot on with these observations. Oh, and in regard to the proper toilet paper orientation, the correct position is the overhang position, at least according to the United States patent (number 465,588, patented December. 22, 1891). Now, go change that toilet paper roll and wash your hands.

NEW YORK, NEW YORK

"Start spreadin' the news, I'm leavin' today." Most of you will recall the start of that song immortalized by Frank Sinatra. Sinatra forever captured the essence of what makes New York, New York, one of the most captivating cities in the world. New Yorkers will of course call it the greatest city on Earth, and, frankly, it would be hard to challenge them on this belief. I have been to New York City in the summer and in the winter. I hope to go again one fall season and one spring season before I leave this world. Some of you may be thinking, "Why would I, in my wildest dreams, want to visit a city of asphalt?" Well, let's see if I can convince you.

New York City, otherwise known as NYC or simply New York, consists of five separate boroughs. These boroughs, Brooklyn, The Bronx, Manhattan, Queens, and Staten Island, all have unique features that magnetize tourists to them, but I'm going to focus just on Manhattan. I have been to all five boroughs, but like most NYC tourists, I spent most of my time in Manhattan.

New York City, the largest and most populous city in America, was the United States' capital from 1785 until 1790. Originally named New Amsterdam, the city received its permanent name in 1664 when the city was under English control and King Charles II granted the land to his brother, the Duke of York. NYC, one of the most visited cities in the world, has as many as eight hundred different spoken languages. It is one of the most culturally diverse cities in the world and is home to the United Nations headquarters.

My family and I love going to see a live performance. The experience, as an audience participant, watching actors and actresses demonstrate their craft is almost indescribable. When the troupe connects with the audience, it is one of those transcendent times that will stay with the spectators forever. In my opinion, the quality of a theatrical performance is measured by how it compares to Broadway. Broadway, an actual street in Midtown Manhattan, houses several theaters that make up part of New York's Theater District. Some of the longest running performances include *The Phantom of the Opera, Cats,* and *The Lion King.* So a trip to New York would not be complete without watching a Broadway show. But, be warned, tickets go quickly. It is best to buy tickets several months in advance for the show you want to see. If you don't have a preference on a show and just want a great deal, then you can purchase tickets on the day of the show.

After you leave the show, the next place you will want to visit is Times Square. You've probably seen this place on television or in a movie. Most of you will recognize it as the location for the New Year's Eve ball drop. Times Square received its name in 1904 when *The New York Times* stationed its headquarters there. The area has been nicknamed the "Crossroads of the World," and you can sense this reputation as you stand in the middle of this vibrant area. As you listen to Sinatra singing, "I wanna wake up, in a city that doesn't sleep," you will understand what he meant by those words. It truly is a surreal experience.

Though Chicago is the official birthplace of the skyscraper, the offspring relocated to New York. Don't get angry, Chicago; you're one of my favorite cities, but you've got nothing on New York. The architectural wonder of the buildings throughout Manhattan is jaw dropping. The older buildings have historical value and interesting stories, while the newer ones show off the technology of the times. You will certainly be able to recognize the iconic features of the Empire State Building, Chrysler Building, and Flatiron Building, to name a few. The One World Trade Center, otherwise known as the Freedom Tower, standing at a symbolic 1,776 feet in the air, is soon to become the most recognized site on this island. Of course, as a tourist or first-time visitor to New York, you need to go inside the Empire State Building. At one time, it was the world's tallest building. With its Art Deco style of architecture, you are able to transport back in time and feel you are in a simpler age. Taking the elevator to the observation deck on the 86th floor will give you bird's-eye views of the city below. Leaving the observation deck, fun diversions wait inside as you escape from King Kong. If you don't get the King Kong reference, go watch the original 1933 movie by the same name. I assure you, you won't be disappointed.

New York City does not disappoint one's palate. Any and every type of food that you would want to eat will be available in the Big Apple. I can't really comment on the fancier, better-known restaurants, as I have never been to one in NYC. However, from what I've been told, they are worth every penny, and they are expensive. This is New York, after all. What I can tell you is that the "street food" bought from vendors is a true culinary delight. We're not just talking hot dogs, but also international dishes that would proudly be served in one of those fancy restaurants.

Of course, the standard fast food and chain restaurants are available for those people that don't wish to stray too far from their familiar fare. I would be remiss if I didn't mention Hell's Kitchen, not the television show, rather an area in Manhattan dense in outstanding and unique restaurants.

A visit to NYC would not be complete if you left the city without eating a deli sandwich and a slice of pizza. Several famous delis are scattered throughout the city. You might need to split a sandwich as some of these delis pile the meat so high on the sandwich, you can't even fit it in your mouth. Being from St. Louis, I believe that we have the best style pizza with our thin, crispy crust, while Chicagoans think their deep-dish pizza wins the blue ribbon. It really depends on your mood at the time. Get in the mood, because New York-style pizza is a true joy to your taste buds. The pizza has a hand-tossed crust with wide slices. Make sure you consume one like a typical New Yorker and fold your pie slice in half to eat it.

After you have filled your belly, it is time to work off those calories by trekking around the city. Get on a ferry, head over to Liberty and Ellis Islands in New York Harbor, and walk around the grounds. On Liberty Island, you will be able to get up close with the Statue of Liberty. As most of you know, the Statue of Liberty was a gift from France. As immigrants arrived in New York Harbor in the late 1880s and early 1990s, the first thing they saw was Lady Liberty standing tall. She was welcoming them with open arms, and they knew, at that moment, that their American dream could become a reality.

After you propel yourself up the stairs inside the Statue of Liberty, you can head over to Ellis Island. Millions of immigrants passed through this island as it housed the

United States' busiest immigration station. Ellis Island no longer serves immigrants, but it does have some remarkable museums. As you wander around the grounds and buildings, you are able to read and hear the stories of that time as the past comes alive before your eyes. If the song Ol' Blue Eyes made famous was around back in the late 1800s, I bet I would hear some people sing "these vagabond shoes are longing to stray." The National Park Service has done a fantastic job of pulling you into a remarkable historical time of our country.

Finally, one site that you must visit is the 9/11 Memorial. I will warn you that, though the site is breathtaking, sadness will overtake your emotions as you walk around these hallowed grounds. But you will leave with a sense of hope, strength, and inspiration. You will come to better appreciate the courage and selflessness of the first responders. You will strengthen your love for our country and the symbol of freedom that we share with the world.

I don't think many people need much, if any, convincing to vacation in New York. I have just touched on a few of the vast opportunities that are available with a visit to the Big Apple. However, some of you city dwellers may not want to visit another city. Rural folk may overlook NYC for fear of being surrounded by skyscrapers and concrete. But sometimes you need to get out of your comfort zone; otherwise you will miss out on the memories our great country has waiting for you.

Lessons Learned From the Movies

I heard a line in a movie once that said that all of the answers in life can be found in the movies. While this could be disputed, movies do reflect vast and thought-provoking views of our culture. I thoroughly love going to the movies or watching a flick in the comfort of my home. A movie allows the viewer to transcend their reality for a short time. A movie may simply be watched as a fun diversion. Other times, movie watching may teach a lesson or expand one's perspective on a topic.

I have picked ten of my favorite movies. You may notice that I didn't list any popular movies such as *Casablanca, Citizen Kane, Star Wars,* or *Caddyshack*, to name a few highly respected movies. I loved those movies, and their value certainly is not to be diminished. I chose the movies below because I learned a valuable life lesson from each and every one of them, and I wish to share that lesson with you. I'm sure that you have your own list, but I encourage you to check these out.

ROCKY (1976, DRAMA)

Main cast: Sylvester Stallone, Talia Shire, Burt Young, Carl Weathers, Burgess Meredith

Plot: Rocky Balboa, a local club fighter from Philadelphia, gets chosen to box against Apollo Creed, the reigning world heavyweight champion.

Lessons learned: This movie moved me in ways that have carried into my adulthood. I learned at a young age that, even against all odds, I should shoot for the stars with my dreams. I was able to incorporate inspirational and upbeat songs into my workouts. I discovered creative and adaptive measures to get the job done rather than making excuses for my situations.

SHAWSHANK REDEMPTION (1994, DRAMA)

Main cast: Tim Robbins, Morgan Freeman

Plot: Andy Dufresne, an innocent man, forms a life-long friendship with Ellis "Red" Redding, a contraband smuggler, while both are incarcerated at Shawshank State Penitentiary.

Lessons learned: I found myself believing that certain criminals can be rehabilitated and, depending on their crime, should be given the opportunity to pay their debt and work toward redemption. I was reminded about the power and strength that a friendship can give to individuals. I was able to visualize on the screen how hope plays out in a dire situation.

Monty Python and the Holy Grail (1975, Comedy/Fantasy)

Main cast: Graham Chapman, John Cleese, Terry Gilliam, Eric Idle

Plot: King Arthur and his Knights of the Round Table go on a search for the Holy Grail.

Lessons learned: I learned how to escape from my reality for a few hours and indulge in relaxation and fun. I came to appreciate parodies and the British approach to some comedies. I learned how to belly-laugh so hard that it hurt.

The Godfather (1972, Crime/Drama)

Main cast: Marlon Brando, Al Pacino, James Caan, Richard Castellano, Robert Duvall

Plot: The Don Vito Corleone Italian-American patriarch is followed as the organized crime family transfers power from father to son.

Lessons learned: I was too young to see this movie when it debuted in 1972. I remember my parents coming home from the theater talking about it. I appreciated the sacrifices and love that a family will offer to one another. However, I came to see how love can be misdirected and misconstrued. I vividly saw how death and destruction are the ultimate endings for evil ways.

Schindler's List (1993, Drama/History)

Main cast: Liam Neeson, Ralph Fiennes, Ben Kingsley, Caroline Goodall

Plot: Oskar and Emily Schindler, a German business-man and his wife, save over a thousand refugees from the Holocaust during World War II.

Lessons learned: What I learned about the Holocaust in school paled in comparison to the three hours that I spent at the theater watching this movie. The atrocities and horror of the Nazi regime burned a desire in me to go through life with love and acceptance. I was instilled with hope and inspiration seeing others risk their lives to help others.

JAWS (1975, THRILLER)

Main cast: Roy Scheider, Robert Shaw, Richard Dreyfuss, Lorraine Gary, Murray Hamilton

Plot: A great white shark gets hunted by the local police chief and his crew after the shark inflicts death and fear among the local beachgoers of a small resort town.

Lessons learned: I learned to respect the unknown and be afraid when I really need to be afraid. I gained a new respect for sea creatures, and it carried with me to my scuba diving days. I was taught that you will ultimately win if you stay on the course long enough.

FERRIS BUELLER'S DAY OFF (1986, COMEDY)

Main cast: Matthew Broderick, Alan Ruck, Mia Sara, Jeffrey Jones, Jennifer Gray

Plot: A high-schooler, along with his best friend and girl-friend, skip school for a day's adventure in downtown Chicago, despite his principal's opposition.

Lessons learned: This movie really helped remind me that the destination is in the journey and that you need to smell the roses along the way in life. Sometimes I need to throw caution to the wind, laugh, and not take life so seriously. Ferris sums it up with his statement, "Life moves pretty fast. If you don't stop and look around once in a while, you could miss it."

ALIEN (1979, SCI-FI/HORROR)

Main cast: Tom Skerritt, Sigourney Weaver, John Hurt, Veronica Cartwright, Harry Stanton

Plot: Terror ensues on the commercial starship *Nostromo* after the crew encounters a mysterious life-form.

Lessons learned: Human beings are as alien to extraterrestrials as we are to them. You don't think so? Just assist on a cesarean section and you will know what I mean. Good or bad, a certain level of respect is due to all living creatures.

PHILADELPHIA (1993, DRAMA)

Main cast: Tom Hanks, Denzel Washington, Roberta Maxwell, Buzz Killman, Karen Finley

Plot: Andrew Beckett, a homosexual lawyer inflicted with HIV/AIDS, hides his illness and sexuality. Once these private matters are discovered by his firm's partners, he is dismissed from the Philadelphia-based law firm.

Lessons learned: At a time when I was in medical school, I saw chilling and disturbing discriminatory actions placed on a man based on situations beyond his control. I was reminded not to pass judgment but rather focus on the healing process. Empathy became concrete in my therapeutic approach to my patients.

THE PASSION OF THE CHRIST (2004, DRAMA)

Main cast: Jim Caviezel, Maia Morgenstern, Christo Jivkov, Francesco DeVito, Monica Bellucci

Plot: Jesus of Nazareth's final twelve hours are followed, up to and including his crucifixion.

Lessons learned: This was neither the best movie I have ever seen nor was it the most enjoyable. But it reminded me why I would die for this man, a man I believe is the Savior of the world.

I could go on and on and give you a lesson learned for every movie I've seen in my life. The lesson may be as simple as a new place, a new look, a new idea, or just a new word. So, next time you watch a flick, give it a try and see what you might learn. You may just surprise yourself.

SUCCESS DEFINED

How do you define success? Dictionaries define success simply as favorable outcomes. If that is true, then is it possible to succeed when you have failed on the outcome? Recall Thomas Edison's quote "I have not failed. I've just found ten thousand ways that won't work." The key to success is to take one step at a time until you find yourself at the top of the ladder. Let's look at different ways that we succeed as human beings.

Every one of us has been successful in our lives. Just look at the progressive nature of infancy. We reach milestones as we transition from infancy to the toddler years. We push on and move into childhood, head into the preschool years, and, next thing you know, we hit the preteen stage. This is followed by the young teen years, quickly fading into the teenager stage, only to be topped by reaching young adulthood. In the first twenty years of our lives, we have succeeded in remarkable ways. We have learned to walk, talk, eat, and think. We have shown the world that we are our own being, a true gift to this Earth.

Success comes in different ways, at different times, and the value of it varies from individual to individual. Goals are certainly the means by which we become successful. In other words, we all must have a directive by which we measure success. Is it my goal to win a soccer game or merely play in one? Is it my directive to become recognized as one of the top physicians in the country or simply give the best care to my patients? Success can result from a task as simple as twisting the lid off a peanut butter jar or as daunting as traveling to outer space. In any case, it is for us to choose our direction in which to succeed.

Success begets success but failure does not lead to failure unless we allow the failure to define us and overcome our existence. As Edison so eloquently pointed out, a failed attempt at something is not necessarily a failure. It becomes a success if we are able to analyze the failure, learn from the mistakes made, and move on to our desired goal. Unfortunately, many people get so caught up in their failed attempt that they do not or are not able to let go. They then get stuck in the middle of their self-directed pathway.

In my senior year of college, I took the Medical College Admission Test (MCAT), a test required to get into medical school. This test, at that time, was a major factor in medical school admission boards' decision for entry into their medical schools. I failed the test miserably and so badly that a monkey could have randomly picked out more correct answers than I had. I had a decision to make after such a dismal performance. Do I pursue my dream of becoming a doctor or give up?

At that time, I was only twenty-one years old, and I had my entire life ahead of me. I was derailed by my disastrous MCAT results, and I had to make a decision and determine how I was going to define my success. I could buckle down and spend every waking hour studying for a repeat test while still salvaging getting into medical school the next fall. However, I chose to forgo the test, and enjoy my senior year. The enrichment and development that I was receiving from my extracurricular activities were too important and significant in my life to pass up.

Five years would pass after college graduation before I would enter into medical school. I still had the goal of becoming a physician in the back of my mind, but I knew that I needed more growth and experiences before I attained such a goal. Remember, success is defined by one's own determined goal, not by others. For me to be a successful physician, I had to become an empathetic, caring individual. Back then, sure I cared about the welfare of puppies, but I was so self-centered and so self-absorbed. I took those five years to mature into adulthood.

Some people will say that I wasted five years, but fortunately it doesn't matter what these people think. If I take five minutes out of my day, and, say, play a video game on my smartphone, have I wasted time? Some will say yes, but I say no. I spent those five minutes enjoying my time; I have also de-stressed my mind, allowing for a more productive day. The same goes with those five years. I took the time to better define myself. I took the time to better prepare myself. I took the time to be successful, not only five years later, but along the course of the five years. I learned from my mistakes and pushed forward.

All that being said, as a Christian, my success is not defined by specific set goals, but rather I am called to be faithful and obedient to my Father. This obedience insists that I love my fellow man and that I follow what I am called to do. That's why I didn't give up on medical school. I believe that being a loving and caring physician was and is my calling from God. What's nice about our callings is that they may change over time. When I was just out of college, God was calling and directing me to develop a stronger foundation before I set my eyes on being a physician. While God has called me to be a physician, he has also called me these days to write and share these words with you. That is why I get up early and stay up late to put my thoughts into words.

The ultimate means by which we succeed should be based on the meaning of life itself. For some, that meaning is, in my opinion, misdirected by means of attaining wealth or power, or by living a luxurious and hedonistic lifestyle. I believe that the meaning of life is to leave this world in a better place than before you found it. True happiness and true success arrive when we give ourselves to others through charitable endeavors. No, that doesn't mean we all have to join a monastery or become a missionary. We give ourselves to the world by discovering what our calling is and then moving in the direction of that calling.

Though the destination may be perceived as the ultimate goal, the journey along the way is how we succeed. If you don't know what you are called to do in life, then listen closely and open your eyes wide. You'll soon hear and see it as vividly as you see the sunshine or the smell scent of blooming flowers.

Now go on your journey with godspeed!

AMUSEMENT PARK
MEMORIES

An amusement park is a place for entertainment. It provides the visitor with a selection of rides, games, eateries, shows, and sometimes themes. Lake Constance, the oldest continuously operating amusement park in the United States, opened in 1846. It is located in Bristol, Connecticut. Bakken (officially known as Dyrehavsbakken) is the oldest continuously operating amusement park in the world. It opened in 1583 and is located north of Klampenborg, Denmark. Undoubtedly the most recognizable and most popular theme park in America, and perhaps the world, is Magic Kingdom at Walt Disney World, located in Lake Buena Vista, Florida.

As we age, disdain and misery come to mind when a lot of us think of visiting an amusement park. For most children and adolescents, heading to one of these places is a dream come true. Traversing through the long lines, large crowds, and sometimes unpredictable outdoor climates are trumped by the exhilaration and sheer joy of the event. I remember daydreaming for weeks on end before my first visit to Disneyland in Anaheim, California. I was also blessed with a Six Flags amusement park being just minutes away from my hometown of St. Louis, Missouri.

It doesn't take much, if any, convincing a child or teenager to spend a day at an amusement park. As adults, some of us keep that spirit alive, while others choose to remember it as a memory. Fortunately, these days, almost anyone can visit one of these parks, as a lot of them have accessibility for those with special needs. I am going to share with you some of the popular amusement parks I have had the opportunity to visit in my life (listed in alphabetical order) and hopefully instill in you the desire to visit one.

BUSCH GARDENS TAMPA BAY

- Location: Tampa, Florida
- Website: buschgardens.com/tampa
- Parent corporation: SeaWorld Parks & Entertainment, Incorporated
- Busch Gardens theme parks are located in Florida and Virginia
- Favorite ride/attraction: Kumba Steel Roller Coaster
- Favorite memory: Seeing my daughter be in awe as she watched the animals roam around in a natural habitat

DISNEY'S ANIMAL KINGDOM

- Location: Orlando, Florida
- Website: disneyworld.disney.go.com
- Parent corporation: The Walt Disney Company
- Favorite ride/attraction: It's Tough to Be a Bug!
- Favorite memory: Seeing the animals roaming freely along the course of a guided African savanna tour

DISNEY CALIFORNIA ADVENTURE PARK

- Location: Anaheim, California
- Website: disneyland.disney.go.com
- Parent corporation: The Walt Disney Company
- Favorite ride/attraction: Turtle Talk With Crush
- Favorite memory: Eating lunch at Ariel's Grotto while my daughter was mesmerized by meeting Ariel

DISNEY'S HOLLYWOOD STUDIOS

- Location: Lake Buena Vista, Florida
- Website: disneyworld.disney.go.com
- Parent corporation: The Walt Disney Company
- Favorite ride/attraction: The Twilight Zone Tower of Terror
- Favorite memories: Feelings of excitement, anticipation, and a little bit of fear as I waited in line to get on the Tower of Terror ride; getting to participate in the original Studio Backlot Tour

DISNEYLAND PARK

- Location: Anaheim, California
- Website: disneyland.disney.go.com
- Parent corporation: The Walt Disney Company
- Favorite ride/attraction: Buzz Lightyear Astro Blasters
- Favorite memory: Seeing my daughter's face glow as she met her favorite princesses during a character meal while being dressed up as a princess herself

Disney's Magic Kingdom

- Location: Lake Buena Vista, Florida
- Website: disneyworld.disney.go.com
- Parent corporation: The Walt Disney Company
- Favorite ride/attraction: Space Mountain
- Favorite memory: Getting dressed in a tutu after being called up to the stage during a dinner show at the Fort Wilderness Resort

Epcot

- Location: Orlando, Florida
- Website: disneyworld.disney.go.com
- Parent corporation: The Walt Disney Company
- Favorite ride/attraction: Canada Far And Wide in Circle-Vision 360
- Favorite memories: Eating lunch in the German Biergarten Restaurant; visiting the Flower and Garden Festival and seeing the look of fascination on my wife's face as she looked at the elaborate topiaries

Knott's Berry Farm

- Location: Buena Park, California
- Website: knotts.com
- Parent corporation: Cedar Fair Entertainment Company
- Favorite ride/attraction: Timber Mountain Log Ride
- Favorite memory: I remember as a child looking up from a distance at the log ride. At the time, it was the biggest, scariest, and highest ride I had

ever seen. I almost chickened out, but I mustered up the courage and had the ride of my life.

Legoland California

- Location: Carlsbad, California
- Website: legoland.com
- Parent corporation: Lego Group
- Legoland theme parks are located in California, Florida, Denmark, Germany, United Arab Emirates, Japan, Malaysia and England
- Favorite ride/attraction: Miniland U.S.S.
- Favorite memories: Building and racing Lego cars with my daughter; shopping for some cool Lego sets in the gift shops; watching my daughter "attend" Driving School in Fun Town

SeaWorld Orlando

- Location: Orlando, Florida
- Website: seaworld.com/orlando
- Parent corporation: SeaWorld Parks & Entertainment, Incorporated
- Sea World theme parks are located in California, Florida, and Texas
- Favorite ride/attraction: Kraken Floorless Roller Coaster
- Favorite memory: Seeing my wife get soaked by a sea lion's splash

SeaWorld San Antonio

- Location: San Antonio, Texas
- Website: seaworld.com/san-antonio

- Parent corporation: SeaWorld Parks & Entertainment, Incorporated
- Sea World theme parks are located in California, Florida, and Texas
- Favorite ride/attraction: Sea Lions Exhibit
- Favorite memory: Visiting my college friends and touching the stingrays at the stingray tank

SeaWorld San Diego

- Location: San Diego, California
- Website: seaworld.com/san-diego
- Parent corporation: SeaWorld Parks & Entertainment, Incorporated
- Sea World theme parks are located in California, Florida, and Texas
- Favorite ride/attraction: Skytower
- Favorite memory: Seeing the smile on my daughter's face as she met and hugged Elmo in person

Silver Dollar City

- Location: Branson, Missouri
- Website: silverdollarcity.com
- Parent corporation: Herschend Family Entertainment
- Favorite ride/attraction: Christmas Lights during *An Old-Time Christmas* festival
- Favorite memories: Visiting the park as a teenager and taking the garter off one of the girls at the Silver Dollar Saloon; taking my wife to a Moonlight Madness night, riding the roller coasters in the dark, and even riding Thunderation backwards; returning with my family with sea-

son passes in hand and visiting all of the festivals one year

SIX FLAGS ST. LOUIS

- Location: Eureka, Missouri
- Website: sixflags.com/stlouis
- Parent corporation: Six Flags Entertainment Corporation
- Six Flags theme parks are located in Arizona, California, Georgia, Illinois, Maryland, Massachusetts, Maryland, Missouri, New Jersey, New York, Oklahoma, Texas, Canada, Mexico, and Saudi Arabia
- Favorite ride/attraction: Screamin' Eagle Wooden Roller Coaster
- Favorite memory: Spending my high school summer days walking around the grounds.

UNIVERSAL STUDIOS FLORIDA

- Location: Orlando, Florida
- Website: universalorlando.com
- Parent corporation: Comcast
- Universal Studios are located in California and Florida
- Favorite ride/attraction: Universal Orlando's Horror Make-Up Show
- Favorite memory: Constantly feeling like I was about to walk into a live movie set.

UNIVERSAL STUDIOS HOLLYWOOD

- Location: Universal City, California
- Website: universalstudioshollywood.com

- Parent corporation: Comcast
- Universal Studios are located in California and Florida
- Favorite ride/attraction: Jaws: The Ride
- Favorite memory: Seeing Grandpa from the Munsters in full costume while eating lunch at the commissary; taking a backlot tour and getting to see the sets where Lucille Ball and Abbott and Costello performed their trade

UNIVERSAL'S ISLANDS OF ADVENTURE

- Location: Orlando, Florida
- Website: universalorlando.com
- Parent corporation: Comcast
- Favorite ride/attraction: Poseidon's Fury
- Favorite memory: Watching my wife, a teacher, enjoying her experiences in the Dr. Seuss area

All fifty states have had an amusement park in their state at one time. I listed only the ones that I have physically been to in my life. I have even had the opportunity to visit some now-defunct parks, such as Dogpatch USA in Marble Falls, Arkansas, and Astroland in Coney Island, Brooklyn, New York. I have some great memories from all the parks I have visited in the past. I am looking forward to packing my bags in the future and taking my family back to Disney World. I also want to pay a visit to the Wizarding World of Harry Potter at Universal Orlando. I'm sure that you have had some fond memories visiting an amusement park at one time in your life. So, either as a participant or spectator, put your walking shoes on, go through the turnstile, and make some lasting memories again.

SOCIAL RESPONSIBILITY VS. PERSONAL FREEDOM

In the wake of the COVID-19 pandemic, I feel compelled to write about our responsibilities as citizens to our society versus our personal freedoms. I thought our society could not be as divided about any topic other than politics, but then the coronavirus pandemic hit the country. I will preface this article stating that I am biased. I believe mask wearing should be a national mandate and that physical (better known as social) distancing should be the norm. That being said, I plan to discuss a balanced viewpoint of one's social responsibilities with one's personal freedoms. I am presuming that the reader agrees with me that the pandemic is real, a threat to peoples' lives, and not a conspiracy of false news.

Social responsibility is the duty that an individual has for the benefit of the society. It is an ethical framework by which one acts to balance their daily lives with the lives of others. We all (or at least most of us) practice social responsibility in our daily lives. We wear clothes out in public, we stop at stop signs, we pull over for funeral processions and emergency vehicles, and we pay our taxes. We further contribute to society based on our individual ethical foundation.

In the corporate world, corporations and businesses act socially responsible by paying their employees fairly and equitably, focusing on ethical business practices, facilitating long-term economic growth, and donating to philanthropic initiatives.

Personal freedom, on the other hand, is an individual's freedom in moving about, court equality, private property security, freedom of speech, and freedom of conscience subject to the rights of other individuals and the public.

Examples of personal freedom include our right to dress in our own style, our right to express our opinions in speeches and writings, our right to vote without oppression, and our right to own property. The United States of America leads the world in allowing society a broad range of personal freedoms. Many of us feel that is what makes America great.

The tricky part of any society is allowing an individual their personal freedoms while balancing out the responsibility that is needed to maintain an orderly state. Governments and corporations have to mandate that certain and specific personal freedoms be given up in order to allow the country or business to succeed and prosper. Let's look at a few examples of how society enforces social responsibility while maintaining an individual's freedom.

We allow adults to drink alcohol, but not while driving. If an individual drinks responsibly, they can enjoy their desire to imbibe alcohol. But if they decide to drink and drive, they are not only risking their own life but the lives of others. Thus it is mandated across our land that an individual cannot drive over a specified blood alcohol threshold. We have found that other means of distracted driving, such as texting or cellphone use, also contribute to societal hazards.

We allow teenagers and adults to drive while maintaining an active driver's license, but our society mandates that drivers stop at red stoplights and stop signs. We all know that traffic lights prevent havoc and chaos, and most of us follow the rules out of social responsibility (or at least to not get a ticket).

A more controversial personal freedom is allowing motorcycle drivers to ride their bikes on the streets without helmets. Some states allow for this personal freedom, while other states mandate that motorcyclists wear helmets. The personal freedom side argues that by not wearing a helmet, it is only the individual who is being harmed. With accepting the risk of potential personal injury or death, the motorcyclist can choose whether they want to wear or not wear a helmet. The social responsibility side points out that, though the individual is the only one physically harmed, society is adversely affected as a whole when a motorcyclist incurs injury without wearing a helmet. The harmed motorcyclist may become disabled, thereby placing a financial strain on society. Other people involved in the motor vehicle incident may feel guilt and remorse for the outcome, even if it was not their fault.

Now let's focus on the specifics of the coronavirus pandemic. It is a social responsibility of every individual to wash our hands after using the restroom and stay home from work when we are ill with an infectious and contagious disease. Yet, prior to the pandemic, studies showed that a significant percentage of the population did not wash their hands. Due to the pandemic, we have advanced this responsibility to include social distancing and mask wearing when in public. However, a large portion of our society believes that their personal freedoms are being infringed upon with mask wearing and social distancing measures.

When we look at the psychology of restricting personal freedoms, we see that people develop strong emotions toward these restrictions. People feel that their civil liberties get violated in certain instances and they will thus fight against the restrictions. This is normal human behavior. It becomes the societal leaders' responsibility to explain to the masses why one's personal freedoms need to be restricted for the welfare of the community. Just think of the outrage many smokers feel about not being able to smoke in public. They have every right to smoke and destroy their own bodies. Society has deemed, however, and from a medical standpoint rightfully so, that they do not have the right to inflict secondhand smoke exposure onto others in public.

Now let's turn to social responsibility. During this pandemic, one has to practice social distancing, wear masks, and stay home when ill. We have enough substantial evidence that these measures help prevent the spread of this deadly virus. Yet our society is confused as our leadership has sent mixed, false, and misleading information to the public. Furthermore, some of our medical organizations have made mistakes along the way, such as initially saying masks were not needed among the public, further muddying the water. This adds fuel to the fire when an individual fights for personal rights. Instead of having a collegial discussion, both groups (mask wearers and non-mask wearers) have opted for violent protests and digging their feet in the sand. Our society has been through a difficult year with sheltering in place, which has been challenging, since we are social creatures; we have yearned for the social interaction we so desperately need.

My family and I have opted to shelter in place since the beginning of spring. We keep our distance physically from others, wear masks in public, and wash our hands frequently. My wife has resigned her teaching position this school year so that she can stay at home with our daughter, who attends school remotely. I wear a face shield and other personal protective equipment (PPE) when I examine a patient.

Look, I get it. I understand that we are all fatigued with the demands that this pandemic forces upon us. I understand the disparity that some feel frightened while others are angry. I realize that some groups feel that their political views are being challenged. If only we could put our differences aside, we would all get a clear picture of what social responsibility means for our fellow person. I hope and pray that we figure it out before it is too late.

O CANADA!

Ever since I visited the Canadian exhibit at Epcot in Orlando, Florida, I have yearned to visit Canada. "Canada Far and Wide in Circle-Vision 360" was a spectacular visual presentation at Epcot by our northern neighbor. So when I had my opportunity, I jumped at the chance, with a day trip to Vancouver, British Columbia. Years later, I wanted to expose my daughter to a different culture, so we packed our bags and took off for Montreal, Quebec.

Canada is the second-largest country in the world, distance wise, with a total population of just under thirty-eight million people. English and French are the official languages. Ottawa, Ontario, is the capital city, and Toronto, Ontario is the most populated city. Canada consists of three territories and ten provinces. The territories are the Northwest Territories, Nunavut, and Yukon. The provinces are Ontario, Quebec, Nova Scotia, New Brunswick, Manitoba, British Columbia, Prince Edward Island, Saskatchewan, Alberta, and Newfoundland and Labrador. Six times zones span the country, including Pacific, Mountain, Central, Eastern, Atlantic, and Newfoundland. Daylight Savings is practiced in every province and territory except for Saskatchewan.

According to the Canada Guide, for 2020, the average life expectancy is eighty-years for men and eighty-four years for women. Cancer, followed by heart disease, is the leading cause of death. Home ownership is around 66 percent. The median annual family income was estimated at $78,870 in 2014 (Canadian dollars). Some 13 percent of Canadians were considered to be "low income" in 2014. Canada's murder rate is around six hundred people per year, and around forty thousand Canadians are incarcerated. Canada ranks twenty-fifth out of 180 countries for environmental quality metrics.

Canadians consist of 80 percent having a European background with the remaining 20 percent being a mixture of every other race on Earth. A very small percentage of natives, or aboriginals, are in the mix, with the remainder of the population being descendants of immigrants or immigrants themselves. Canadian law followed the parliamentary supremacy principle until 1982, when a new section called the Charter of Rights and Freedoms was added to the Canadian Constitution. This gave way to improved human rights for the citizens.

Children are legally required to attend school from the age of 5 until 18, or from kindergarten through twelfth grade. The public school system provides free education. Some Canadians advance to higher learning institutions. The economy is largely made up of the service sector, in which up to 75 percent of Canadians are employed. Trade is the largest component of Canada's Gross Domestic Product, and the United States is the largest importer of Canadian goods.

Canada's money system is similar to that of the United States but consists of the Canadian dollar. Bills are in 1, 5, 10, 20, 50, and 100 dollar incremental values. Canadian coin values include the loonie (one dollar), toonie (two dollars), quarter (twenty-five cents), dime (ten cents), nickel (five cents), and penny (one cent). These coins are produced by the Royal Canadian Mint.

The Canadian military system consists of the Canadian Army, the Royal Canadian Air Force, and the Royal Canadian Navy. With one of the smallest militaries in the world, Canada has about fifty thousand military personnel.

Enough about the basics of the Canadian structure; let's now focus on my memorable experiences in Canada. Hopefully, I will be able to entice you to yearn for a visit to this breathtaking country. I'm going to focus on my Quebec trip, but I'm sure all the provinces and territories have the perfect vacation for just about anyone.

Since I became a father, I have wanted to expose my daughter to different cultures and ways of life. I want her to grow up feeling connected to all walks of life. One way we are able to do this is to visit different countries. Each year we try to pick a different country to visit, and so far we have been to China, Cuba, Canada, Jamaica, and the Bahamas. For the most part, Canada is not much different from America, at least on the surface. But the Quebec province has a distinct French European flare. When we visited Canada a few years ago, my daughter really wanted to go to France. Not wanting to spend so much money or take so much time getting to our destination, I suggested we pack our bags and head to Montreal, Quebec, Canada.

We chose to visit Canada in the summertime when the average maximum temperature is 77 degrees Fahrenheit. We stayed at the Marriott Springhill Suites at the edge of Old Montreal, which was ideal for our family. The first night I accidentally stumbled into a historic restaurant,

Le Auberge Saint-Gabriel, for our first meal in Quebec. Auberge Saint-Gabriel, built in 1688 by a French soldier, was the first "auberge" to receive a liquor license in North America back in 1754. Not only was the food delicious, but I was struck in awe of this building's magnificent architecture. From the onset, I knew this vacation was going to be special, enriching, and memorable.

We are churchgoers, and so we started Sunday morning off with mass. This mass was special in that the service was spoken in French at the Basilique Notre-Dame De Montreal. While I didn't understand a word the priest said, I actually understood the entire mass. This may be one of the top basilicas in the world with its ornate stained-glass windows, impressive grand organ, and commanding Gothic Revival architecture. Completed in the 1800s, the minor basilica is a designated National Historic Site of Canada. Situated in the historic district of Old Montreal, this wonderful work of man is not to be missed, even by the non-religious.

We spent a large chunk of our time exploring Old Montreal and the Old Port. Old Montreal, located between the St. Lawrence River and the downtown skyscrapers, was founded in 1642 and once walled off as a fortified area. From what I have been told, you feel, and I did, like you are in France as you walk around the narrow streets and hear French being spoken in the background. We shopped at the many stores along Rue Saint Paul (Montreal's oldest street) and Rue Saint-Amable. We explored Place Jacques Cartier, Place d'Armes, the Old Sulpician Seminary (the oldest standing building in Montreal), Champ-de-Mars, Vieux Port, and Chateau Ramezay. We ate at several of the outdoor seated restaurants, rode in a horse-drawn carriage, and set sail for a boating excursion on the St. Lawrence River. We were immersed in the French-Canadian culture, and it was spectacular.

For transportation, we utilized Montreal's subway system, Montreal Metro, as well as the Montreal Hop-On Hop-Off bus tour. We found the subways to be clean, easily accessible, and safe. We spent two days on the double-decker bus, visiting the following sites: L'Oratoire Saint Joesph Du Mont Royal, Chinatown, Centre Des Sciences De Montréal, downtown, Mount Royal Park, and McGill University. With the Metro, we explored the Underground Montreal City, and were transported to Espace Pour La Vie Montreal in Parc Olympique. While at Parc Olympique, we visited the Biodome, La Tour De Montréal Observatoire, Insectarium, and Jardin Botanique.

Yearning for more of the French-Canadian culture, we took a guided day bus voyage to Quebec City. Quebec City, a three-hour drive northeast of Montreal, is worth a vacation stay in itself. We were able to walk around Old Quebec, North America's oldest streets designated as a UNESCO World Heritage Site, and National Battlefields Park, where the 1759 Battle of the Plains of Abraham took place, when French troops lost to the British in a defining confrontation between the two empires. We visited Chateau Frontenac, the most photographed hotel in the world, rode in a historic funicular (a steep cable railway system), climbed the scenic stairway for a viewing of Montmorency Falls (a waterfall thirty meters higher than Niagara Falls), ate lunch at an outdoor restaurant, and stepped through one of the opened Holy Doors at the Notre Dame De Quebec Cathedral Basilica. This truly is a magical and gorgeous city.

Canada is rich in history, diverse in culture, and beautiful in its land. The Canadian people are warm and inviting. The United States is truly blessed to have our northern friends as our neighbors. It would behoove us all to go visit them sometime.

MUSIC MOVES US

Music moves me, and I would bet with absolute certainty that music moves you, too. The studies in psychology are on my side, so much that my bet with you would be unethical; that is, I'd be betting on a sure thing. Music is so ingrained in our lives that a lot of us take it for granted. We listen to music when we are happy. We listen to music when we are sad. We hear music in the background of television shows, commercials, movies, and even when we listen to talk radio. We are touched by music consciously as well as subconsciously. Let's look at ways that music moves all of us.

Who among us has not heard or sung the "Happy Birthday" song? This song is likely the most popular and most sung song in the English language. The song sparks happiness and joy to the recipient as well as the singers. Some studies suggest that the song enhances the palate, thereby making birthday cake taste better. It is the easiest song to remember, and medically, we advise singing it twice for the proper hand-washing duration. The song can be sung at any age. If we are not singing it in our homes, we hear it at our workplace or restaurants. Like the saying, "It's five o'clock somewhere," chances are, someone in the world is singing this song right as you are reading these words.

Children thrive when they are exposed to music, with songs ranging from nursery rhymes, to set music on a show, to original songs from artists. Growing up in the 1960s and 1970s, I remember hearing music while I watched *Sesame Street, Schoolhouse Rock!,* and *Mister Rogers' Neighborhood.* I embraced Disney songs like "The Bare Necessities" and "When You Wish Upon A Star."

The 1980s rolled in with Disney songs still being popular among children and adults. *Kids Incorporated* was popular then. This show integrated music to address serious child and adolescent issues.

The late 1980s and 1990s brought us boy bands like New Kids on the Block and the Backstreet Boys as well as that purple dinosaur, Barney.

After the turn of the century, we listened to songs from *The Wiggles* and *The Fresh Beat Band.* Parents are well familiar with names like Laurie Berkner and Dan Zanes. I could go on and on with popular children's songs and groups, but the point is that children love music.

After we leave our childhood and adolescent years behind, we still find a way to bring music with us on our life's journey. The soundtrack of the movie *Rocky* inspired me so much that I would crank up my Walkman, toss in the cassette, and set out on my runs in order to stay in shape for my own boxing career. Athletes and health aficionados use music to dance better and move more, and to elevate their workouts to reach a new level. We feel pumped up and more powerful with the correct song choice.

Once we are done working out, most of us like to relax. What better way to calm our bodies than by listening to soothing music? Sitting by the fireplace with a book in hand as we listen to classical or new age music allows me to decompress from the day's stressors.

Some people may say "Bah!" or "Yuck!" to classical music. Yet as they watch that scary horror flick or suspenseful crime drama, their emotions are enhanced by that very same music. Unbeknownst to the movie viewer, an orchestra is playing that eerie or mysterious music in the background, adding an element of excitement to one's senses.

Music moves us even when we are sad. This may be a time when we need music the most. Studies even show that sad music touches us in ways we may not even realize. We are able to connect with someone, the songwriter (or more likely the singer), who expresses their own sad feelings in verse. We use the song to trigger memories, memories that are uplifting, important, or significant in our lives. We depend on music to make us feel good or to distract us from our blues.

We celebrate our love for our Supreme Being in song. If you are Catholic or Christian, your church services will integrate music into love and devotion for the Holy Trinity. Not only does the choir belt out beautiful and inspirational songs, but the congregation contributes their voices as well, while the church interior is blasted with a euphonious tone. Non-Christian religions also incorporate music into their devotions. Even non-religious people are moved by songs such as "Ave Maria" or "Hallelujah."

Have you ever been to a professional or college sporting event without hearing a song at some point during the game? In most countries, the national anthem is played before the game starts. We all rise and belt out "Take Me Out to the Ball Game" in the seventh inning of baseball games. My favorite hometown hockey team, the St. Louis Blues, embraced "Gloria" during our glorious and memorable race to winning our first Stanley Cup. College sports love music. When basketball players foul out, fans sing lyrics to "Na Na Hey Hey Kiss Him Goodbye." Football team bands will bang out six notes and then the fans will shout out "Charge!" Even if an athlete mocks the arts, these same people are the ones singing at the top of their lungs while rooting on their team.

Western weddings typically start with a processional wedding song as the bride comes down the aisle. Another song is typically played at the end, as the married couple walks out together. The reception often consists of a live band with a lot of the participants celebrating the couple's commitment in song and dance. When attending weddings, I find myself, a non-dancer, out on the dance floor caring little about my awkwardness and dance ability.

Schools have integrated music into their curriculum. Students who participate in the performing arts typically perform better on standardized testing. Integrated music in classrooms will enhance the students' learning by decreasing anxiety, improving concentration, and helping the regulation of their emotions. We know from research that music affects our brain in positive ways. Businesses have figured this out; that's why they pipe music into elevators, overhead in their stores, and on the telephone when we're placed on hold, all in an effort to soothe the customer. During my thirty-five-minute work commute, I often switch on the radio to some fifty's music or Ol' Blue Eyes, Frank Sinatra, for a calming effect.

Music crosses all languages and touches everyone. Coincidentally and also symbolically, I hear music as I am writing this line. My wife and daughter are watching *America's Got Talent* on television. As I look up, a ten-year-old Canadian singer has moved forward in the contest, and last year's winner, an autistic blind man, is singing a beautiful and moving song. Whether you like it or not, as Gloria Estefan noted, the "Rhythm Is Gonna Get You."

HOLIDAY MEMORIES

Holidays are a special time for many of us. Often, we are given the day off from work, and we look forward to spending the day with family and/or friends. Some of us spend weeks and months in preparation, and we are exhilarated with the anticipation as we wait for the days leading up to the event. Below, I have listed the main American holidays along with some of my fondest memories of that holiday.

NEW YEAR'S DAY

- January 1
- Enjoying the day off from work while relaxing with the family, doing absolutely nothing or playing some board games
- Sitting around the television set watching a college football bowl game
- Eating black-eyed peas, grapes, maybe kale for that good luck superstition, but saving the collard greens for the family
- Working out a new exercise regimen to start off the New Year
- Taking that family winter vacation: one year to a tropical setting and another to snow-covered mountains

Martin Luther King Day

- Third Monday In January
- Showing respect and giving homage to a man that led us in the direction of diversity, equality, and freedom for all
- Sitting down to read about this wonderful man
- Participating in a day of service to our community
- Attending one of the celebratory festivals around the country
- Enriching our lives with a visit to a history museum

Valentine's Day

- February 14
- Taking my sweetheart to a romantic dinner at a fancy restaurant
- Bringing home a beautiful bouquet of flowers and card for my wife
- Drawing up a warm bath and transforming the bathroom into a spa-like setting. OK, I've never done this for my wife, but I think about doing it every year; maybe this year the idea will finally become a reality
- Going on an overnight road trip
- Spending time with the two girls (now women) I love the most, my wife and daughter

St. Patrick's Day

- March 17
- Celebrating the day on River Street in Savannah, Georgia, at one of the largest St. Patrick's Day gatherings in the United States

- Calling my cousin up and wishing her a happy birthday. Is there someone you know and love who was born on this day?
- Going to a restaurant for an authentic Irish meal
- Surfing the internet reading about St. Patrick and Ireland
- Attending a St. Patrick's Day parade and feeling Irish for a day

Easter

- Date varies determined by Computus
- Dyeing Easter eggs and then taking the kids to an Easter egg hunt
- Having a delicious and fancy Easter brunch
- Attending mass with an elaborate celebration of the true meaning of this day
- Watching my child be astonished with the treats left by the Easter Bunny and recalling my childhood Easter morning days doing the same thing
- Visiting the Easter Bunny wherever he has hopped to

Mother's Day

- Second Sunday In May
- Showing my mom how much I love her
- Watching my daughter give her mother a gift that she designed and made especially for her mama
- Taking the family out for a nice Mother's Day meal
- Letting my wife do whatever she wants on this day
- Bringing home another bouquet of flowers for my wife and for the entire family to enjoy

MEMORIAL DAY

- Last Monday in May
- Remembering the fallen military personnel and thanking our veterans for their sacrifices
- Surfing the internet to read about our American history
- Firing up the grill for a delicious and healthy meal
- Heading to the community pool for a refreshing splash in the water
- Packing up the car and taking the first trip of the summer

FATHER'S DAY

- Third Sunday In June
- Remembering and honoring my father, rest his soul, while reminiscing about the fond memories we shared together
- Knowing that I am who I am because of my father's influences and thanking him for being in my life
- Getting to be the recipient of gifts and love from my daughter
- Going out for a nice meal at a restaurant of my choosing
- Spending time with my family

JUNETEENTH

- June 19
- Celebrating the realization that our country officially determined slavery to be wrong and that

it should always be condemned, no matter the circumstance

- Working to unite our brothers and sisters of all colors together for a better world
- Showing love and acceptance to our fellow human beings
- Taking the time to read about civil liberties and basic human rights
- Learning from our country's past mistakes and progressing forward

INDEPENDENCE DAY

- July 4
- Attending a Fourth of July celebration
- Watching the fireworks display after the sun sets
- Grilling outside but this time with hot dogs and hamburgers
- Having the day off to spend time with family
- Eating my kid's red, white, and blue food item that she baked

LABOR DAY

- First Monday in September
- Celebrating time off from work with a day of rest and relaxation
- Playing a round of miniature golf outside with the family before the cold weather closes the courses down for the winter
- Spending the day with the family at the pool one last time before the pools close for the season
- Another excuse to grill out
- Taking that last summertime vacation before the fall season hustle and bustle sets in

BIRTHDAY

- September 14
- I consider my birthday a holiday; maybe you can convince your boss to let you have your birthday off
- Celebrating me and my existence; being narcissistic for a day
- Getting the family to do what I want to do this day
- Taking a day off from work, watching a movie, and going to an arcade for some fun
- Extending the birthday celebration to birthday week; yes, it really is a thing we do. We celebrate the entire birthday week. Why should the greatest day of the year be celebrated for just one day?

HALLOWEEN

- October 31
- Remembering my childhood years—getting dressed up as my character of choice that year and going trick-or-treating with my brother and parents
- Participating in an adult scavenger hunt around downtown St. Louis with my college friends while being dressed up as a vampire
- Handing out candy to the neighborhood kids and seeing all their neat costumes
- Seeing the smile on my daughter's face as she sorts out all of her sweet treasures that she received while trick-or-treating; having her throw me a bone when she gives me a piece of candy that she doesn't want or like

- Watching a scary movie and enjoying being frightened for a few hours

Veterans' Day

- November 11
- Thanking our veterans for their service and sacrifices
- Visiting one of our National Cemeteries
- Paying it forward by doing an act of kindness for someone
- Purchasing goods from a veteran-owned small business
- Attending a Veterans' Day parade

Thanksgiving

- Last Thursday In November
- Having a Thursday off for relaxation and family time
- Indulging in a delicious traditional Thanksgiving Day meal with all the fixings
- Watching the Thanksgiving Day parade on television or attending a local one
- Sitting down with family to watch a Thanksgiving NFL football game
- Welcoming Fred, our Elf on the Shelf, back into our home for the upcoming Christmas season

Christmas Eve

- December 24
- Helping my daughter put out cookies and milk for Santa Claus

- Sitting down by the fireplace while opening our Christmas presents
- Having an enjoyable, fun-filled Christmas Eve house party with family and friends for a memorable night of food, drink, and fellowship
- Watching a Christmas-themed movie. Sometimes we would watch an old throwback like *A Charlie Brown Christmas* or a newer classic such as *National Lampoon's Christmas Vacation*
- Kissing my wife under the mistletoe

CHRISTMAS DAY

- December 25
- Staying up late and attending midnight mass
- Waking up early to see what Santa Claus has brought us
- Seeing the smile on my daughter's face when she discovers the gifts left behind by Santa Claus
- Enjoying the day off work while relaxing with the family
- Heading to the airport for that special Christmas break vacation

NEW YEAR'S EVE

- December 31
- Attending a New Year's Eve party or throwing one of our own
- Reading my past journals that I've kept for a stroll down memory lane
- Watching a year-in-review show, college football bowl game, and/or New Year's Eve party on television

- Getting rid of any unneeded clutter that has collected in the house over the past year
- Outlining my aspirations and goals for the upcoming year

BY THE GRACE OF GOD

As many people ponder over the purpose of their lives, I believe the answer to this puzzling question has already been given to us. I believe we were created by a benevolent God. Our Supreme Being put us on this Earth in order for us to love one another. I deviate from my fellow Christians in that I believe our God will offer eternal salvation to any individual that has demonstrated a Christian life.

I have always struggled with the view that non-Christians or those that do not claim Jesus as their Savior will be forced into the fires of hell for eternity. I don't believe that you can buy yourself into Heaven by doing good works; however, I also don't believe that simply claiming Jesus as your Savior gets you a golden ticket, either.

Now I know that there are Christians reading these words and ready to correct me by stating that is exactly how you get a golden ticket into Heaven. Some of you will also want to tell me that you know with absolute certainty that you are going to Heaven simply because you accept Jesus Christ as your Savior. I certainly respect your belief, and I will accept it as factual if you can prove it to me.

The nice thing about beliefs is that they are ours to hold on to, nurture, and protect. We own our beliefs, but they can be altered by our life experiences. I do believe that I am saved only by the grace of God. I also believe that God's grace extends to Christians, Muslims, Jews, agnostics, the Eastern religions, and even atheists. Unfortunately, one's beliefs can be disrupted, distorted, or destroyed by negative factors randomly or systematically placed on them.

In regard to factual information, we do know that Jesus Christ was a human being. We know that he had many followers, and that he died a horrible excruciating death on the cross. We also know that his body was laid to rest in the guarded tomb; for Christians, including myself, we believe that he was resurrected back to our Holy Father. Other religions will point out that he was certainly a prophet but not a Savior. Even others will push the envelope and say he was simply a man and nothing more.

My Heavenly Father sent his Son, Jesus Christ, to show the world how to live their lives. For us humans, it was kind of a school lesson on how to love, show respect, and pass kindness on to our fellow humans. Back when Jesus walked the land, there was no television, internet, or telephone to be used in order to pass on the word to others in distant lands. So, did those who did not hear about Jesus coming to save us get sent to eternal damnation when they died? For that matter, does a child or adult in today's day and age that grew up with no contact from Christian believers get sent to hell as well?

My belief system holds that my God is an all-loving and benevolent God. I also believe that my God looks at the belief system of the individual and how they carried out that belief in their lives. For instance, for a Muslim adult that has been taught their entire life that their belief foundation was the way through the gates of Heaven, how do they come to trust the Christian evangelist's views? Some may dig their feet in the sand and stay strong to their beliefs because they feel that the Christian is leading them astray. This is also true vice versa, where the Christian may feel the same way toward the Muslim evangelist.

Many Christians are now probably thinking, "You fool! Read your Bible," stating that the answer is inside its pages. Perhaps, but there are different interpretations to the Bible, and it will be hard to convince me that my benevolent God would send someone to the fires of hell simply because that individual chose to follow a different belief system.

Jesus Christ was truly a light to this world. He showed humankind, not as a supreme being, but as a human being, how a man should and must show love for his fellow man. He demonstrated to us the ultimate sacrifice by giving his life for us so that we may be saved. Now, I believe that we were already saved by the grace of God, but Jesus showed us the responsibility that we have to have in order to stay in God's grace.

I know several people who go to church regularly, claim Jesus as their Savior, yet live a hedonistic and destructive lifestyle. Are they truly going to Heaven? Perhaps, but I'm not the decision maker. What we don't know about our fellow people is all of their life's experiences, as well as how they have been affected by their past. A person may be living with several demons in their life, dealing with many difficult struggles and finding that their beliefs are rocked to the core.

Now take a Chinese person who practices Buddhism or Taoism and lives an exemplary "Christian" life; is this person headed to hell? First, we have to define what it means to be Christian to answer this question. We may come up with different answers, based on our own beliefs, and our own or our religion's interpretation of the Holy Bible. I have read the Bible five times and studied it both from my Catholic viewpoint and from my own vantage point. I believe that they will enter into Heaven if they accept that Heaven's entry is only by the grace of God and not by their own works.

Furthermore, I believe that anyone can see the pearly gates if they accept the grace that God has bestowed on us and that they stay in God's grace. So, while good works will not get us into Heaven, they will allow us to stay in God's grace, thereby following the trajectory toward Heaven.

So, what does all this babble mean, and why even write about it? Because it is important to me to convey to you how significant I believe love and kindness are for humankind. That may be pointing out the obvious, but I believe that is how we stay in God's grace. Hatred and evil ways lead to destruction and misery for our fellow people and will cause us to fall from God's grace. The best way to live one's life, no matter what religion you are, is to follow along the path of virtue, love, and kindness, with respect for our fellow beings.

DANCING THE NIGHT AWAY

I despised dancing growing up. When I was in high school, I attended most of the school-sponsored dances, but I was always frightened that I might be asked to join someone on the dance floor. Unfortunately, I was a fairly shy kid, at least around girls. Besides, the girls couldn't find me anyway, as I cowered awkwardly in the shadows with my male friends. I came to find out no one really danced at those gatherings anyway, at least in the eighties.

I later found myself in college, finally mustering enough courage to ask women to dance. I still didn't enjoy the actual dancing, but I did somewhat enjoy the atmosphere. By the time I was in college, I wasn't so self-conscious about my body. Then a movie came out and changed everything. The movie *Footloose* starring Kevin Bacon hit theaters my freshman year. I didn't really have any intention or desire to see the flick, but my college dorm buddy wanted to see it. I was the one with the car, so I said I would go with him. I probably did it just to get away from the stench of our beer-soaked hallways.

So, I later found myself sitting in this theater with my college pal, a gruff, manly man. I felt like this movie should be more of a date-type movie, but I did not care because the movie was fantastic. We danced all the way from the movie theater to the car. We even ended up dancing around the dorm. The cool thing about dancing is that it doesn't matter how good you are—well, unless you're trying to win a contest or make a career out of it. Fortunately for me, I just wanted to dance for the simple joy of dancing.

Dancing allows us to express ourselves. My friend and I danced because we were demonstrating how rejuvenated we felt after watching the movie. The movie had an influence on us that day. This art form allows people to express their emotions by conveying their feelings to others through movement. Dancers can connect with the audience in a way that they may not be able or willing to do otherwise. Dance is used in ceremonial rites and celebrations, notably in Native American cultures.

Dancing has many health benefits as well. The most obvious benefit is that the activity gets our body moving. We are meant to be active, and dancing allows our cardiovascular system to get a good workout. This movement can count toward the one hundred and fifty minutes of our minimal weekly recommended physical exercise. By moving our bodies, we can be able to lose weight, increase energy, improve endurance, strength, and flexibility, decrease stress, improve self-esteem, and be happier overall.

The nice thing about dance is that almost anyone can participate in this activity—the young, the old, the chronically ill, and even the wheelchair bound. It just takes finding the appropriate form of dance for each individual. Let's explore some popular forms of dance styles.

BALLET

Ballet is, in my opinion, the most eloquent and sophisticated form of dance. It is a formal academic-style theatrical dance that combines costumes, music, stage scenery, and the dance technique, the *danse d'ecole*. Ballet originated in the Italian Renaissance as a court entertainment. *The Nutcracker,* associated with Christmas, is probably the most popular and best-known ballet.

BALLROOM

Another form of dance that began in Italy, ballroom dancing quickly spread across Europe and eventually the world. Some of the more popular styles include the cha-cha, tango, and waltz. This is a social dance performed by couples using specific memorized steps. Ballroom dancing was once reserved for the elite social classes but now has spread to every sector of society. Ballroom dance lessons are a popular classroom activity for couples wanting to learn to dance together.

CONTEMPORARY

This style of dance was developed in the twentieth century with elements of ballet and modern dance. As this dance form is more of a philosophical expression, some may refute the above comment. In any case, this is a beautiful fluid type of movement that requires a well-conditioned and athletic body. Recent dance shows such as *World of Dance* have brought this dance style into the limelight.

COUNTRY AND WESTERN

Country and Western dance combines many dance styles often set to country music. Country Western dance can actually be traced all the way back to the tribal rituals of Africa. In America, it has become an adaptation and combination of traditional immigrant cultures. This style of dance is meant to be a social dance activity. Popular styles include line dance, contra dance, square dance, and clogging.

TRADITIONAL (FOLK)

This form of dancing is a reflection and representation of one's culture. It combines elements of music and cultural heritage. Since the middle of the twentieth century, the term folk has often been avoided as it is thought to have a negative connotation. Some popular styles of this category include the Hawaiian hula dance, African gumboot dance, Asian belly dance, Cuban casino dance, Brazilian samba dance, and Irish step dance.

HIP-HOP

Hip-hop dance sprung up in the 1970s by street dancers as a way to express themselves to the music of the same name. The hip-hop movement was created by African Americans, Latino Americans, and Caribbean Americans in the Bronx, New York City. Popular forms of this dance style include break dancing, popping and locking, funk, boogaloo, reggae, and uprock.

JAZZ

This performance dance technique can be traced back to African ritual and celebratory dances of the seventeenth century. In America, it allowed Black slaves, ones brought to the United States, a means to express themselves and keep their culture alive. Jazz was made popular by the big band era of the 1930s and 1940s. Popular jazz dance styles include Charleston, Black bottom, and swing dance, such as the jive and the jitterbug.

LATIN AMERICAN

This is a collective dance tradition of Mexico, Central America, and portions of South America and the Caribbean. It is a broad term that encompasses a large group of dance styles ranging from ballroom dancing to traditional dancing. Popular Latin dances include the New York salsa, Argentine tango, Dominican Republic merengue, and Cuban mambo.

MODERN

This theatrical dance developed in the late nineteenth century in Europe and the United States as a rebellious protest to the rigid adherence of classical ballet. Though relying heavily on ballet steps, modern dance is a more free-form style. Modern dance has emerged to include a combination of dance forms. It is a mesmerizing dance to watch, allowing dancers to express themselves by emphasizing their creative choreography and performance.

TAP

Tap dance is a dynamic percussive form of dance in which the dancer wears shoes affixed with metal taps on the toes and heels and taps out rhythmic sounds on the floor. Tap dance finds its origin in the United States, where it evolved from ethnic percussive dance traditions. Tap was made popular by vaudeville and is still popular today.

Dancing is a part of our human culture. Dance allows us to express ourselves, bond with others, celebrate our culture, and promote health. There are hundreds of other dance styles and variations not listed above, yet they are all worthy in their own right. It looks like it is time now to put on your dance shoes, be footloose and fancy-free, and dance the night away.

Eat to Live or
Live to Eat

There are those individuals who eat only to sustain life, while others live only to indulge in the pleasures that foods and drinks provide. The key to successful healthy eating is to combine the two elements, thereby engaging in a pleasurable eating pattern as a means to sustain life.

Like many Americans, I have struggled with this necessary balance. I love to eat, but I also love to do other things in my life. I like to hike, I like to bike, I simply like to move. However, when I indulge too much, I just want to sit.

Unfortunately, our society is packed with overweight and obese adults. The Centers for Disease Control and Prevention (CDC) states that the obesity rate in 2018 was 42.4 percent and the severe obesity rate was 9.2 percent in America. Almost three in four men and two in three women are over the normal weight range. Over 25 percent of adults do not engage in any leisure-time physical activity. The current minimum recommendation for children and adolescents is one hour of vigorous activities per day, and for adults, it is one hundred and fifty minutes of moderately vigorous activity or seventy-five minutes of vigorous activity per week. Muscle-strengthening activity recommendations are three and two times per week for adolescents and adults respectively.

Bear with me as I give you some background information about myself, as I suspect a lot of you share similar stories. I was a very active child and young man. I participated in organized athletics from elementary school until college. I maintained my weight by being an active boxer and wrestler, though in retrospect, my weight was probably not healthy; I was always trying to shed a few pounds in order to make the weight limit for my bouts. Coaches back in the 1980s would push athletes to lose anywhere from a few ounces to several pounds on the day of the match. In any case, I stopped boxing after my first year in college and gained the "freshman 15" that so many college kids do. Through the years, my weight yo-yoed with wide weight fluctuations. I was able to maintain a healthy weight for weeks to years, but I always regressed back to an obese state. Even after having medical consequences from my weight, I still continued to stay at an unhealthy weight.

Being a physician, our profession is full of highly focused, driven, intelligent, and task-oriented individuals. We have excelled in our studies, and we work hard in order to optimize the care of our patients. We have the urge and desire to be in control of our lives and our surroundings. Our society has marked us in the past as having a god complex, in which we feel like a god and believe we are unable to do any wrong. Though I have never felt that way toward others, I have unfortunately felt that god complex towards myself. I felt like I was in complete control of my life and that it was only up to me to correct any of my shortcomings and misgivings. These feelings and attitude have contributed to my very unhealthy weight.

I had the intellect to realize these shortcomings, but I continued to ignore some of them. I became angry when my medical community defined obesity as a disease. I held a belief that obesity could be overcome by simply eating less and moving more. I presumably gave my patients all the necessary tools to overcome obesity, but I often would overlook the root of the problem. I have come to believe that obesity is a disease state, affected by personal, environmental, and societal influences that can alter one's physical, emotional, and spiritual balance. Though I still believe that weight loss can be attained by following the simple concept of increased activity and caloric restriction, the obese state is much more complex than that principle.

So what is happening in our society that causes our overweight and obesity rate to skyrocket over the past fifty years? It is not simply that we are intentionally lazier than our predecessors, but we have been trained through the years, due to societal influences, to live a more slothful, sluggish lifestyle. The instant-gratification culture has led our minds to believe that we can have anything and everything at our fingertips as soon as yesterday. This mindset extends to thinking we can lose weight without any effort, shedding several pounds within days.

When I was growing up, drive-thru fast food was not readily available, but now a drive-thru restaurant is on almost every street corner. Our restaurant-served food portions have tripled in size. Large groups of people have migrated to the suburbs from the cities, and the means of transportation has shifted from walking and bike riding to driving and using public transportation. Instead of going outside to play and wander the neighborhoods, children are often now corralled inside for play dates, due to the fear of stranger danger. Playing football or tennis has transformed from actually doing it on the field or court to playing it on a television or video screen.

Furthermore, with the obesity levels that we have reached, we have activated certain receptors and genes in our DNA that promote obesity. We eat processed foods that do not keep us full and also leave us wanting more. This all sounds like a doomsday scenario, but there is hope and help available for those individuals who are willing to work for a healthier body.

I would be remiss if I tried to tell you how to lose weight in a few paragraphs. Some people can do it on their own. Others may need the help of their physician, while some may need the multidisciplinary team approach with their physician, nutritionist, trainer, counselor, support groups, and/or obesity specialists. If you are overweight or obese and don't know how to safely lose weight, the best place to start is with your physician or health provider. Any respected and knowledgeable primary care physician, nurse practitioner, or physician's assistant can help lead you in the right direction.

I will be frank with you and tell you that I am on a journey of obesity recovery, as I am now on a downward (that's good) trend with my weight. I was at one time so severely obese that I did not want to do anything but eat and sleep. After reading the writing on the wall, I knew I was headed to the remainder of my days being filled with misery and an early demise. I chose to change my course, and I started with baby steps. I downloaded an app on my phone that allowed me to do chair exercises. I have since progressed to, once again, riding my bike and exercising on my elliptical machine. I choose to portion-control my diet with the assistance of the NutriSystem program; this may or may not be the right program for you. The bottom line is that I chose to change my trajectory, and you can, too. This pathway is by no means an easy one. If it were, then we all would be at our ideal body weight—fit and trim. I have been successful by clinging onto the Alcoholics Anonymous saying that I can do it for one day. If I can't do it for one day, then I can do it for one hour, and if I can't do it for one hour, I can do it for one minute. Those minutes will turn into hours, those hours will turn into days, then weeks, and then months. Next thing you know, you have reached one of your success milestones. Now, go seize the day.

Hobbies: Pleasurable Diversions

The definition of a hobby is a pleasurable activity that is practiced or participated in outside of a person's normal occupation. This diversion is for many a pursuit meant for relaxation, while for others the goal is stimulation. I have found my hobbies to be enriching and rejuvenating, allowing me to focus more intently as an active physician. While watching television can certainly fit under the hobby category, I hope that you will want to participate in a hobby that is more stimulating to either your body or your brain.

Listing hobbies would, in theory, result in an almost infinite number. I have listed, in alphabetical order, some of the hobbies that I have participated in as well as some of the more popular hobbies. In any case, it behooves you to choose a hobby, not only for the sake of relaxing, but to expand your mind, body, and soul.

ANIMAL THEMES

- Animal rescue — This can range from volunteering at an animal rescue facility to adopting a pet of your own. My family has rescued several family pets.

- Aquariums — Our aquarium has been the home of two gerbils, some snails, and several fish.
- Beekeeping — Not only do you get to dress up in a cool suit, but you just might get some honey to eat as well.
- Bird-watching — With proper research, you'll be looking at the trees in a whole different light.

ARTS AND CRAFTS THEMES

- Candle making — This always seemed like a fun thing to do when I watched my daughter dip a stick in hot wax at the amusement parks. We would then come home with a rainbow-colored candle.
- Coloring — This has long been a popular pastime for children, and now adults can do it, too, since so many adult coloring books are being published.
- Drawing — The nice thing about this one is that no talent is required. If your family lets you, you can even try drawing on the walls.
- Jewelry making — This can be a fun way to make some extra cash.
- Knitting — I'm always excited when I'm the recipient of the knitter's finished product, unless the item has three arms.
- Model building — This was one of my favorite pastimes growing up and it remains so now that I am an adult. My wife made me throw out all of my scaled model cars, but I took photos so they will stay with me forever.

- Painting — Every few years, I will purchase one of those paint-by-numbers kits to feed my need to paint. My daughter, however, has better skills than me and can paint without the numbers.
- Pottery — We still have the pieces that my daughter made when we attended ArtsFest in Springfield, Missouri.
- Soap making — The final product can be a gift or an item to sell as long as it doesn't take the skin off the user.

COLLECTIONS THEMES

- Antiquing — Even if you don't collect these or can't afford to, it is still cool to rummage through antique shops to find some treasures.
- Coin collecting — I passed all of my childhood coins I collected to my daughter. It was cool watching her look at them the other day. In my opinion, all children should have this hobby for at least a short time in their lives. It can start with just looking through a roll of pennies for that one wheat penny.
- Card collecting — I still have all the baseball cards I collected as a child. Maybe some of the cards are worth something, but it doesn't really matter because they are all priceless to me.
- Genealogy — This is a fun way to research your family's past.
- Records — I wish I would have kept my collection of vinyl records from my childhood.
- Scrapbooking — My wife really got into this hobby the first five years of our daughter's life. It

seemed like I was always accompanying my wife to the scrapbook store.

CULINARY THEMES

- Beer making — My college friend thoroughly enjoys this hobby, or maybe his real hobby is drinking the beer.
- Cooking — I like to hang around these people, once they have perfected their craft.
- Grilling — I like to grill healthy chicken, fish, and vegetable choices most weekends throughout the year. I'm like the post office; rain, sleet, sun, or snow won't stop me from firing up the grill.
- Wine tasting — This is a nice group activity, as you can socialize while practicing your hobby.

DO-IT-YOURSELF THEMES

- Car restoration — My dad always surprised me in that he owned an auto parts machine shop, but on the weekends, he loved tinkering with the engine of the car he was restoring.
- Carpentry/woodworking — I had a patient who created masterpieces I couldn't afford.
- Furniture restoration — You'll be able to turn that previously thrown-away desk into an heirloom.
- Gardening — The flowers can be put in your vase or stay outside to share with others. The food grown can be thrown on the grill or taken to your cooking class.

GAMING THEMES

- Board games — My daughter always defeats me when we play *Beat the Parents*.
- Chess — Not only is the game fun, but it stimulates the brain.
- Darts — I was never that good playing this bar game until I found a dart game app on my smartphone. Now I just need to transfer my smartphone gaming skills to the dartboard on the wall.
- Magic — Mesmerize your audience with a spectacular performance.
- Model trains — What a cool way to combine my childhood memories with model building.
- Poker — This is a very popular hobby that has made some amateurs a lot of money.
- Pool — Be a shark and stay on the green slate the entire night.
- Puzzles — Sitting in a cabin on a cold winter day is a fun time, especially when you do a jigsaw puzzle together.

LITERARY AND ARTISTIC THEMES

- Dancing — You can take a class or simply head out on the dance floor to get your groove on.
- Instrument playing — There are several instruments to choose from out there; just remember you can't carry a piano around.
- Photography — Pictures really do say a thousand words.
- Poetry — I've always wanted to sit in and listen at one of those New York poetry recitals.

- Reading — I love reading nonfiction and fiction books. Too cheap to buy books, I read off my wife's book list. Fortunately, we have similar reading tastes.
- Singing — My daughter has latched on to this activity. Thank goodness she can sing, and oh, my, can she sing.
- Theater — You can be part of the backstage team, an usher, or the lead role.
- Writing — I'm participating in one of my favorite hobbies now.

OUTDOOR THEMES

- Camping — The last time I went camping it rained about four inches that night, but we still had a trip to remember.
- Fishing — Ah, I remember those days I spent fishing off the Back River Fishing Pier in Savannah, Georgia. I never caught anything, but I have vivid relaxing memories of those days.
- Hiking — This is probably one of the most relaxing yet exhilarating and physically rewarding hobbies.
- Hunting — This is not my cup of tea but it sure is for millions out there.

SERVICE THEMES

- Societal organizations — You've got the Elks, the Freemasons, the Kiwanis, and many more, but my choice is the Knights of Columbus.
- Volunteering — The choice is yours, and your volunteering efforts can range from churches to schools to your favorite organization.

Sports and action themes

- Archery — This one involves hitting the bullseye that marks the spot.
- Bowling — I never could get a perfect 300 score, but I did make it to 267 once.
- Coaching — You can lead your team to victory, or more importantly, teach your athletes some valuable life lessons.
- Cycling — Once you learn how to ride a bike, you never forget.
- Golf — Golf courses are always picturesque, breathtaking settings.
- Martial arts — You get to wear a black belt once you prove yourself on the mat.
- Paintball — In the 1970s, our version of this hobby was with water guns. Now they have these elaborate settings and intricate paint guns.
- Rock climbing — You can climb a rock wall inside or a real cliff outside.
- Scuba diving — I made it to the divemaster rating before I gave up this expensive hobby.
- Skiing — You can do this either on the water or in the snow; either way, it's made up of the same substance.
- Surfing — I did this once in my life while in Hawaii. I couldn't stay on the board, but the scenery was breathtaking.
- Tennis — This is an enjoyable activity where you don't want to end up with love by your name.
- Working out — This activity is a great way to stay in shape, relax, and enjoy your free time.

TECH THEMES

- Blogging — A lot of people have turned their passion into a career. But remember that while what happens in Vegas stays in Vegas, what gets put on the internet stays on the internet forever.
- Drone flying — I bought this cool drone about a year and a half ago and still have yet to fly it for fear I'll break it.
- Online courses — There is a course out there for everyone's taste.
- Stargazing — You can really appreciate the night-time sky's beauty when you get away from the city's lights.
- Video gaming —Parents need to make sure they approve of the game, and kids need to do their homework first before throwing a touchdown on the screen.

TRAVEL THEMES

- Cruising — I'm hoping to take a cruise to Alaska one of these days.
- Group tours — We had a memorable heritage tour to China a few years ago.
- Vagabonding — I wanted to do this the summer between college but choose to stay home and make some spending money instead; what a missed opportunity.

Now remember, this isn't an exhaustive list, so don't be writing to me and informing me that I forgot the greatest hobby known to human existence if I didn't list your favorite hobby. If you have a special hobby, keep enjoying it. If you are looking for a hobby, I hope this list gives you some ideas.

EXPERIENCE THE SEASON YOU ARE IN TODAY

Let's talk about seasons—winter, spring, summer, fall. Every one of them is my favorite in its own right. I used to yearn for fall, but as I grew older, I learned to appreciate every day. Everyone seems to be in a rush to be somewhere better than where they are today.

In the frigid days of winter, I would dream of being on a warm beach. Yet in the dog days of summer, I would envision a cold snow falling. As I now have fewer days left on Earth, I absorb every minute of the day and appreciate it for what it is. So, here are some highlights of why I love every season, and I hope that you do, too.

WINTER

- First-day-of-the-year celebrations and rejuvenations after staying up past midnight watching the New Year Ball drop in Times Square
- Sitting by the fireplace reading a good book with a cup of tea with your dog by your side on a cold frigid day

- Grabbing the family, heading out the door with a sled in hand, and making memories on a snow-covered hill
- Going ice skating at an outdoor skating rink
- Watching the Super Bowl and actually looking forward to the commercials
- Building a snowman and having a snowball fight
- Watching Christmas movies, particularly *It's A Wonderful Life* and *A Christmas Story*
- Playing board games or piecing together a jigsaw puzzle with family members
- Hearing the Salvation Army bell ring while walking into a department store
- Going to a large downtown department store and gazing at the elaborate window displays
- Sitting in a hot tub outside as the air temperature falls below freezing level
- Attending a hockey game rooting on your favorite team, or better yet, America's team, the Stanley Cup champion St. Louis Blues
- Taking your sweetheart to that special restaurant for a romantic dinner on Valentine's Day
- Exploring the neighborhoods while looking at all the extravagant Christmas light decorations
- Sipping on some hot chocolate or eating a hearty bowl of homemade soup
- Taking a photograph of the landscape on a sharp, clear day
- Grabbing the family and taking a train ride to the North Pole on the Polar Express
- Celebrating Lunar New Year by attending a festival or parade, shopping at a local Chinatown, or having dinner at an Asian restaurant

- Visiting a greenhouse, rainforest, or tropical setting at a city garden, like the Climatron at Missouri Botanical Garden or Jewel Box in Forest Park (both in St. Louis, the greatest city on Earth)
- Skiing on the slopes at a vacation destination or a local man-made ski slope

SPRING

- Attending an opening-day professional baseball game, especially America's team, the World Series champion St. Louis Cardinals
- Planting a garden in your back yard
- Having a delicious lunch at an outdoor cafe
- Riding a bike on a city trail, country road, or just around the neighborhood
- Flying a kite on a windy day
- Visiting your local zoo and seeing the newborn baby animals
- Going outside on a warm, rainy day without an umbrella, jumping in the puddles, and bringing back those fond childhood memories
- Taking photographs of the budding trees and newly blossomed flowers
- Picking some flowers and bringing the springtime into your home
- Selecting some healthy vegetables and perusing the goods at the local farmers' market
- Heading out to the park for a picnic with the family or loved ones
- Sprucing up the house with a thorough spring cleaning
- Going to a playground and swinging on the swings, no matter what age you are

- Dyeing Easter eggs, watching the kids go Easter egg hunting, having an Easter brunch, and getting a photo with the Easter Bunny
- Planting a tree on Earth Day or Arbor Day and helping keep the environment clean
- Pranking someone, safely and responsibly, on April Fool's Day
- Boating in a lake with a paddleboat or canoe
- Taking a spring break vacation somewhere you have always wanted to go
- Having a good old-fashioned competition with a game of miniature golf
- Drawing on your driveway with sidewalk chalk

SUMMER

- Swimming in your back yard, neighborhood, or community pool
- Visiting an art, history, or science museum
- Attending an outdoor church service, play, or concert
- Going to the movies in an air-conditioned theater or an outdoor drive-in
- Making some homemade ice cream and eating it before the sun melts it
- Packing up the suitcase and heading out for that memorable summer vacation or weekend road trip
- Catching fireflies at nighttime, taking a video of them in your collection jar, and then freeing them back into the wild
- Getting a pedicure and then showing off your toes by wearing flip-flops

- Blowing bubbles outside and then trying to catch them intact on your bubble wand
- Building a sandcastle at the beach or in your sandbox
- Grilling out freshly picked vegetables
- Roasting marshmallows and making s'mores over an open fire
- Learning how to ski or perfecting your waterskiing moves
- Taking a nap in a hammock
- Tossing a frisbee, hitting a golf ball, or serving a tennis ball at the local park
- Lying in a freshly cut grassy field, feeling the sun on your face, and watching the clouds whisk by in the sky
- Rocking in a rocking chair outside while drinking a cold glass of iced tea, and rubbing the glass' condensation on your forehead
- Running through a sprinkler on the hottest day of the year
- Eating fresh watermelon or sucking on a watermelon popsicle
- Strolling through a sunflower field and taking that perfect photograph of a sunflower

FALL

- Attending a tailgating party for your favorite college or professional football team
- Driving around town or hiking in the woods or a park and looking at all the beautiful fall foliage
- Picking a pumpkin from a pumpkin patch and then carving it for Halloween

- Going to a fall festival and picking out that perfect art, craft, or plant for your home
- Dressing up for Halloween trick-or-treating or to attend a Halloween party
- Watching the baseball World Series and rooting on your team
- Renting a cabin at a secluded area or lodge and absorbing the beauty of the surroundings around you
- Raking up the fallen leaves and then jumping into the leaf pile
- Riding on a hay wagon, then warming up next to an outdoor fire with some hot apple cider
- Gathering the family together for a Thanksgiving Day meal, watching the Thanksgiving Day Parade, and catching a Thanksgiving Day NFL football game
- Creating an outdoor fall-themed decoration for your front porch
- Geocaching or scavenger hunting, setting out for that hidden treasure
- Baking a fresh fruit- or nut-filled pie and sharing it with the neighbors
- Sitting by the fireplace or in a rocking chair and knitting a sweater or crocheting a blanket
- Traversing a corn maze without backtracking
- Walking your dog for a longer time and enjoying the moment with your furry friend
- Volunteering at a soup kitchen, local food pantry, or group of your choosing and making it a regular activity in your life
- Getting started on a resolution and making your new habit a routine by the start of the New Year

- Taking photographs of the changing leaves and taking photographs of the same things in each season of the year for comparison
- Spicing up the house with fall-scented candles, sprays, and potpourri

You may certainly prefer one season over another, but make sure you smell the roses along the way. By living in the moment, you'll not only have more vivid memories, but you'll appreciate today for today and not wish for tomorrow.

SMARTPHONE APPS
FOR THE AGES

As a child and a younger man, I was always excited and eager to obtain the newest technologies. In my childhood home, first came the remote control, then the Walkman, followed by the video home system (VHS), video cassette recorder (VCR), and digital video disc (DVD).

I felt like I was tech savvy. When Apple came out with the iPhone in 2007, however, I balked at the idea of a smart-phone. I was amazed at all of the people waiting in line to get one. My flip phone was adequate; besides, who was going to play a game or watch a show on a telephone screen? I figured there would be too many flaws in the first version, so why spend a fortune on one? Fast-forward to 2009, and I'm counting down the days to get my iPhone 3.

Since that time, I have upgraded every one to two years, and now I have an iPhone II Pro. The phone is essentially attached to my hip. I have downloaded thousands of free and paid applications (apps). I currently have 299 apps, 908 videos, 108 songs, and 17,841 photos on my iPhone. Needless to say, I have embraced this form of technology. I feel compelled to share my top twenty favorite apps with you, in no particular order; they are listed and described below.

I will preface by saying that there are thousands of similar apps to the ones I have listed below, and your final choice may be personal preference. Just because an app has five stars (top rating) doesn't necessarily mean that's the app for you. This is simply a guide.

LOSE IT!

This calorie counter app helps the user be accountable for his/her daily food intake. The features include a barcode scanner, photo logging, a nutrients tracker, fitness app syncs, a huge food database, meal planning, motivational challenges, habit patterns, app personalization themes, and workout guides. This is one of the first apps I downloaded. I opted to save money over time by purchasing a lifetime premium subscription.

FITLIST

This workout fitness app allows the user to log and track their workouts as they are working out. It eliminates the need for a written journal log. You can pick from a list of exercises or create your own. The app has several additional features that I have yet to tap into, but I'm satisfied with just using the logging feature.

WEATHER MATE PRO

Sometimes, all you need is to check the temperature on the weather app that comes factory installed with your smartphone. Other times, you might want a detailed forecast and weather information. When the latter occurs, that's when I turn to Weather Mate.

USA TODAY — NEWS: PERSONALIZED

OK, this was a toss-up, as I have eleven news apps installed on my iPhone. I find myself going to this news program over the others as I like to read the national and top stories.

AMAZON

I try to buy my goods locally as much as I am able, but I will use this app as a comparison to see if I can save a lot of money on larger purchases. Since I have an Amazon Prime membership, I will make routine purchases on the fly with free shipping. And yes, I do recycle all of the boxes I receive from them.

CHICK-FIL-A

Since the coronavirus pandemic, I have embraced mobile pay and curbside pickup. I have several restaurant and fast food apps for this exact purpose. Chick-fil-A rises to the top of the list since their food is delicious and their service is second to none.

MASS TIMES FOR TRAVEL

This is basically an app for Catholics, but anyone can certainly use it. When I am on vacation or wish to attend mass at another church, this app gives me mass times near me, as well as directions and parish website links. Now you have no excuse to miss mass while on vacation or if you can't make it to your parish's mass time.

GASBUDDY: FIND & PAY FOR GAS

I loathe overpaying for gas, but I also won't drive ten miles trying to save a few bucks. This app allows me to find a gas station just around the corner where I may be able to save several cents per gallon. I'll check it before heading home from work when I need to fill up my tank.

LYFT

I really appreciated having this app the last time we went on vacation. We were able to find a ride within minutes at locations that didn't have typical taxi services on standby. We also saved about a hundred dollars in taxi fees. If you aren't aware of Lyft, it is a public transportation service where you hail a ride and pay for it, along with any tips, directly from your smartphone.

YAHOO SPORTS: WATCH NFL LIVE

This is another one of those categories where I have several apps specific to all of my favorite high school, college, and professional sports. This app gives me reliable and accurate up-to-the-minute updates on scores, news, and standings of different sports.

1 PASSWORD

With all of the worries of identity theft and being a victim myself, I keep all of my passwords safe in this protected password app vault. The app is user friendly, and I am able to categorize my protected passwords.

MERRIAM-WEBSTER DICTIONARY

A dictionary is an essential reference to have by your side, but no one wants to lug around a heavy book anymore. This app puts the dictionary and thesaurus right at your fingertips.

TINY SCANNER PLUS

I no longer scan documents the old-fashioned way. I simply pull out my smartphone, open this app, and snap a picture of my desired document. I can then send and save the scanned documents. I don't use this app all that often, but when I need it, it really comes in handy.

YELP FOOD, DELIVERY & SERVICES

I have downloaded countless apps in this category of searchable services and food businesses. Yet this is the only one that still remains on my iPhone, whereas all of the others have been deleted. The only thing I need to start doing more is looking at the reviews before I sit down to eat and not while I am waiting for the food to arrive at my table.

5 MINUTE CLINICAL CONSULT

This is my biggest category collection, as I have forty-two medical apps on my iPhone. Though I use my UpToDate subscription the most, this medical app is a quick user guide. Though expensive (it is priced at a hundred dollars), it is an excellent resource for basic medical information. It is geared for the medical professional, but the layperson will find it valuable as well.

GRATITUDE ROCK JOURNAL

I keep a weekly gratitude journal of the main things I have been grateful for in the previous week. This app allows me to text my thoughts and take up to three photographs with each entry. I print out the journal at the end of each year and review it on a regular basis in order to keep me thankful for what I have in my life.

WORDS WITH FRIENDS 2 WORD GAME

I, like many smartphone users, love to play games on my phone, especially while I'm waiting in line or taking a break. I love this Scrabble-themed game with its variations. Not only is this game a nice diversion, but I am able to fulfill my competitive nature. I also feel like I am stimulating my brain and learning some new words along the way.

IMDb: MOVIES & TV SHOWS

When I can't remember performers' names or movies that they have been in, or even if they are still alive, I can always count on this app to find me my answer. This is an awesome source for movie, television, and celebrity information.

CAMERA

One of the main reasons that I purchased a smartphone is that I am able to have a camera available at my fingertips. With over 37,000 photographs downloaded onto my computer, I love to capture the moment with a picture. I have tried multiple camera apps, but I always seem to come back to the factory-installed one. Maybe it is because I'm not a professional photographer and need the simplified version, but this app gets the job done for me.

INFORMANT 5 CALENDAR

OK, I admit it. I saved my most favorite app of all time for last. This is a versatile and detailed calendar app that, in my opinion, blows the competition away. I use it as a journal, and I am able to record details of my daily events in less than ten minutes. I print out the calendar each month and save it in a folder as a nice reference of what once was in my life; that way, the few words I saved spark my memory and allow me to vividly recall a specific day in the past.

You may have noticed that I didn't mention such apps as Facebook, Twitter, TikTok, or Instagram. While I have two of these apps on my smartphone, they are just no longer my cup of tea. Ironically, the app I despise the most on my iPhone is the actual phone app. I guess I'm old school, but I enjoy talking on a landline phone so much more than on cell phones. Well, time to wrap this up so I can check out the new selections on the app store.

LGBTQIAPK+: Letters in the Alphabet and an Oppressed Group

When I was growing up, the acronym LGBTQIAPK+ didn't even exist. But then again, "LOL" also had no meaning back in those ancient times. During my childhood and youth, alternative lifestyles were frowned upon. The military had the "Don't ask, don't tell" policy, the gay community was accused of creating the AIDS epidemic, and gay men were bullied by being called "faggot" and were beaten to death just because of their sexuality. A certain code existed in society, and if someone deviated from these artificial restrictions, then resistance and hatred would befall the individual.

Times have since changed, some for the better, some for the worse, but they have changed nonetheless. So, what exactly does LGBTQIAPK+ mean? The acronym stands for Lesbian, Gay, Bisexual, Transgender, Queer/Questioning, Intersex, Asexual/Ally, Pansexual, Kinks, and other non-heterosexual people.

As a medical professional, though there are only two main human genetic identities (male and female), variations exist in the genetic code that affect the hormonal and physical balance of individuals. The rarest form of gender identity is a hermaphrodite (outdated term), a living being with both male and female reproductive organs. Most humans will either be born with two X chromosomes or an X and Y chromosome. Still, there are others who will have mosaic genetic variations with cells having both XX and XY chromosomes in their genetic makeup. From a scientific standpoint, we have not identified any specific gene that determines a person's sexual orientation. We only have theories at this point, believing that sexual orientation is complex, with genetic, hormonal, and environmental factors influencing the outcome.

Though I am a heterosexual, I'm going to describe the LGBTQIAPK+ acronym from my perspective. I have progressed over time with my acceptance of these nontraditional sexual orientations. Growing up, I was led to believe that these ways of being were misguided, inherently wrong, sinful, and frankly evil. It was thought that the gay movement's objective was to convert all of the heterosexual people into homosexuals. While I no longer believe that a person's sexual orientation is evil or inherently wrong, it really doesn't matter what I believe, as long as the person is not being manipulated or coerced into their beliefs and actions. We live in a country that has fought wars and defended our citizens' rights of freedom and expression. So why would we want to condemn an individual who wants to love and feel love from another human being, just because we are not copacetic with it?

The term "lesbian" describes a female-identified individual who is attracted to another female-identified individual in a romantic or erotic manner. An emotional connection may exist between the two people, or the desire may simply be sexual. When I was younger, this group was lumped into the category of homosexuality. The term lesbian was adopted from the feminist movement of the 1960s and 1970s.

The term "gay" replaces the word homosexual, as the latter word has had too many negative connotations. Initially, the word simply meant to be happy or cheerful. Over time, the word has come to describe mainly male-identified individuals who are attracted to other male-identified individuals in a manner similar to the term lesbian. It also can mean any individual who does not identify as a straight person. The term "straight" is reserved for an individual who has an attraction to the opposite sex. Another term for straight is "cisgender."

The term "bisexual" is used to describe an individual who is attracted to either males or females. Some will say that the definition refers to being attracted to all genders. This group was once ostracized by some as having the identity of oscillating between being straight and gay. This viewpoint is not only inaccurate, but it contains an assumption that may be emotionally damaging to those individuals.

The term "transgender" describes those individuals whose gender identity, gender expression, or both differs from the sex that they were assigned at birth. These individuals may opt to transform their bodies hormonally and/or surgically, or they may simply dress in the gender opposite their assigned birth sex. Some also choose not to express their identity through outward indications like clothes. Crossdressers, however, do not necessarily fit under this category. Transgender is an umbrella term for this group that was once called transsexual. The transsexual term is no longer used; however, this group may sometimes be called "trans."

The letter Q in LGBTQIAPK+ stands for both "queer" and "questioning." When I was growing up, the word queer was a derogatory term to describe the gay population. Today, for some, it is morphed into a more pleasant term describing being part of the LGBTQIAPK+ community. The term questioning refers to those individuals who are trying to figure out their place in the LGBTQIAPK+ community.

The term "intersex" is an umbrella term for an individual who is born with ambiguous sexual or reproductive anatomy. These people may have external female characteristics but have internal male anatomy, vice-versa, or a variation of both sexual characteristics. This term reflects a spectrum of biological variations.

The term "asexual" refers to those individuals who do not feel a sexual attraction to other individuals. This is another umbrella term that exists on a spectrum. The asexual spectrum consists of a sexual orientation and a romantic orientation. Asexual people may or may not be celibate and may or may not have a romantic attraction to someone.

The term "ally" refers to those individuals who are supporters of the LGBTQ+ community but do not themselves identify as a member of this group.

The letter P stands for "pansexual." The pansexual individual is a person who has a sexual, romantic, and emotional attraction to someone, regardless of their biological sex, gender, or gender identity.

The term "kinks" refers to those individuals that have sexual fetishes that are out of the ordinary, according to the general population. This may include such fetishes as bondage or spanking.

The "+" symbol refers to several other different sexual orientations and gender identities that are not described in the lettered acronym. This list is ever growing, and the acronym is slowly being added to; the LGBTQIAPK+ acronym initially started out as LGBT. The plus sign symbolizes the acknowledgement that a person is free to identify as whoever they choose to be.

While all of these descriptions may be confusing, they reflect the view that a person is free to have his/her own identity. If I offended anyone or have missed anyone's identity, I apologize, as it certainly is not my intention. Whether or not you agree with the terms listed above, it is important to acknowledge that we are complex human beings. By understanding where a person is coming from, we will be able to bridge the gap between people, and love them for who they are and not who we want or think they should be.

A Cuban Adventure

Back in 2019, I traveled with my family on a cruise to Key West, Florida, and Havana, Cuba. I wanted to get my daughter to Cuba once the travel restrictions had been lifted so that she could get a glimpse of a different culture. This was before the deadly coronavirus pandemic, a pandemic that would forever change travel cruising. Below is our itinerary.

Day 1 — Monday, March 11, 2019

Our departure was from Port Everglades in Fort Lauderdale, Florida. My family and I boarded the *Majesty of the Seas* at 1 p.m. This is a Royal Caribbean ship that holds approximately 2,500 people. We spent the afternoon at sea. Multiple and diverse activities were available to occupy our time and educate and entertain us. Our ship had restaurants, pools, a rock-climbing wall, a gymnasium, a spa, theaters, bars, lounges, shops, and a casino. I managed to hit a royal flush playing video poker, allowing me to gamble on the ship's dime for the remainder of the cruise.

Day 2 — Tuesday, March 12, 2019

We spent the day at sea. While my wife and daughter spent most of the day lounging by the pool, I explored the ship's fourteen decks. I walked around the multiple decks, attended two lecture series on Cuba, played blackjack in the casino, and read in the Viking lounge on the top deck with the vast ocean visible below. My family and I met up for meals. Food was available almost 24 hours a day.

DAY 3 — WEDNESDAY, MARCH 13, 2019

Land ho! We arrived in the morning at Key West, Florida. We disembarked at 8:30 a.m. with the family setting foot on land for the first time in two days. We planned ahead, as land excursions are limited in time, and we had many options from which to choose. We opted to explore the island on our own, as we felt comfortable on U.S. soil. We rode on the World Famous Conch Tour Train to get a historical perspective of Key West, have a mode of transportation, and be able to hop on and off the train at our leisure. We headed for a photo op at the Southernmost United States Point Marker, then walked over to Ernest Hemingway's home for a tour and to spot the polydactyl cats roaming around the grounds. After some gift shopping, we ate lunch at the RoofTop Cafe. We headed over to Kermit's Key West Lime Shoppe as our cruise director noted this as a place for all things related to key limes. We ended our Key West excursion with a visit to the Key West Aquarium. That evening, we saw a 1970s themed show in the ship's theater, then headed to dinner.

DAY 4 — THURSDAY, MARCH 14, 2019

We arrived in Havana, Cuba, in the morning as it is only ninety miles from Key West, Florida. We opted for the ship's sponsored excursions for all of our Cuba adventures. Our morning excursion was the Havana by Classic American Car tour. Havana is speckled with over 60,000 American-made 1950s automobiles, most of which serve as taxis. In a pink 1954 Chevy convertible, we toured Havana, driving by El Capitolio and down El Malecon, a seaside avenue, where we passed by the Miramar neighborhood, Verdado District, and Paseo Del Prado. We stopped off at Plaza de la Revolucion, where Fidel Castro, popes, and dignitaries have given historic speeches. Our next stop was the Hotel Nacional de Cuba, where we traversed the grounds and drank mojitos. Several celebrities have stayed there through the years, and this was the site where five hundred mafia family members held a meeting that was featured in the movie *The Godfather*. After finishing our refreshing mojitos, we stepped onto a luxurious bus and were taken to Callejon de Hamel, where we were given an overview of Santeria, an Afro-Cuban-based religion. We ended our tour by walking through Old Havana, passing by Plaza de Armas and Plaza de la Catedral.

After having lunch and relaxing on the ship for a few hours, we set out for our evening excursion. We chose the Panoramic Night Tour. This was a combined walking/bus tour. We again toured Old Havana and Hotel Nacional de Cuba and saw Havana lit up at night. We drank mojitos at Ernest Hemingway's hangout bar, Bodeguita del Medio. Though most of the buildings are in need of repair, we were still able to appreciate the beautiful architecture that exists throughout the city.

DAY 5 — FRIDAY, MARCH 15, 2019

This was our last day in Havana, giving us time for a morning excursion. We selected the Easy Panoramic Havana

Tour. We drove down El Malecon, visited the Plaza de la Revolución, then headed to see some new sites. We stopped off at Fusterlandia. This is a unique art community where the Cuban artist Jose Fuster has covered the area with intricate tile mosaics. This is also a great shopping opportunity to bring home some memorable trinkets. We then headed to El Morro Castle. Construction on this castle began in 1590 and was completed in 1630. It was strategically located at the entrance to Havana Bay. We ended our tour at El Cristo de la Habana. This is a 20-meter tall statue of Jesus Christ overlooking Havana. The monument was made in Italy by Cuban artist Jilma Madera. From this location, we could see our ship, Havana Bay, and the Havana skyline. That evening, our ship made the trip back to Fort Lauderdale, Florida.

DAY 6 — SATURDAY, MARCH 16, 2019

We arrived at Port Everglades in Fort Lauderdale, Florida, and disembarked at 8 a.m. We opted to take an evening flight back to Missouri so that we could spend the day in Fort Lauderdale. I wanted my daughter to see old Florida, so we spent a few hours at the Flamingo Gardens Botanical Gardens Wildlife Sanctuary. After taking a tram tour and walking around the gardens, we headed to Bob Roth's New River Grove for some refreshing freshly squeezed orange juice. After enjoying a relaxing drive up the A1A Coastal Byway, we ate lunch by the ocean at Sea Watch Restaurant in Lauderdale-by-the-Sea.

Our family voyage to Cuba was a success. My goal was twofold: have a relaxing and enjoyable spring break with my family while setting out to see a culture worlds apart, yet steps away from the United States. Though Cuba is a socialist country and starkly differs from our country's form of democracy, her people are full of love and principles. The Cubans we met along our journey welcomed us with open arms and showed us, in a glimpse, their zest for life.

SADNESS IS NOT A WEAKNESS

When a baby is born, we are all excited for the family. We throw baby showers for the parents and we go visit the baby and parents in the hospital. When a person dies, we send our condolences with flowers and cards. We also attend the funeral of the deceased. When a family member or friend is ill with a physical ailment, such as pneumonia or a fractured bone, we wish them well and bring food and other comfort items to their home.

When a person is hospitalized due to a mental illness, we avoid them. We keep quiet and act like nothing happened. Our society views mental illness more as a weakness than an illness. This viewpoint is not unique to the United States, as it is present in many other countries. This misconstrued belief needs to be changed, and it starts with opening a dialogue.

When I was in my medical training, I was so severely depressed that I simply wanted the pain and anguish to go away. I never had a specific suicidal plan, but I had ideations of my car driving off a cliff or heading into oncoming traffic. I had the insight to seek counseling, but I downplayed the seriousness of my illness. I probably should have been on an antidepressant, but I feared the consequences pharmacologic treatment would have on my career. Fortunately, I did not self-treat with alcohol or illicit drugs. Instead, I worked through my major depressed illness with my counselor, and I have not suffered from a depressed state since that time. Though my depression was situational, it was severe and disabling. I did not need to suffer as much as I did during that time, but the stigma of having a mental illness outweighed my desire to seek proper treatment.

Our overall health is determined by a healthy balance of our physical and mental health. Physical ailments, such as chronic medical conditions like heart disease and Type 2 diabetes, can increase the risk of someone developing a mental illness. Likewise, people afflicted with mental illnesses are at an increased risk for having chronic medical conditions. Mental illness is one of the most common health conditions in the United States. The Diagnostic and Statistical Manual of Mental Disorders, Fifth Edition, (DSM-5), published by the American Psychiatric Association (APA), lists and gives the diagnostic criteria for specific mental illnesses. Though the list is beyond the scope of this article, some common mental illnesses include depression, anxiety, bipolar disorder, and schizophrenia. Mental illnesses can occur in adults, children, and adolescents.

THE CENTERS FOR DISEASE CONTROL AND PREVENTION (CDC) NOTES THE FOLLOWING STATISTICS:

- More than 50 percent will be diagnosed with a mental illness or disorder at some point in their lifetime. One in five Americans will experience a mental illness in a given year. One in five children, either currently or at some point during their life, have had a seriously debilitating mental illness. One in twenty-five Americans lives with a serious mental illness, such as schizophrenia, bipolar disorder, or major depression.

In the earlier days of our country, state psychiatric health facilities were referred to as lunatic asylums. In my younger days, mental illnesses were not even really discussed in the public arena. A larger percentage of people suffered with impaired mental health in silence. If a person became so disabled that hospitalization became necessary, their social circle typically referred to them as crazy, since they were admitted to the loony bin. They would even say they had gone off the deep end. Movies like *One Flew Over the Cuckoo's Nest* and *The Shining,* though great movies in their own right, further stigmatized this belief.

Since I have entered the medical environment as a medical professional, I have seen a positive shift in the manner and attitude in which people with mental illnesses are processed through the medical system. Back when I was in training, if Prozac (Fluoxetine) didn't improve a patient's mental health, physicians quickly consulted a psychiatrist. We would lean on psychologists for assistance and counseling, but all too often, the patient's health insurance would not cover mental illnesses, and the patient could not afford the counseling services.

The medical community felt and sometimes made it known that patients with mental illnesses drained them physically and emotionally. As time progressed, our society has worked to de-stigmatize the affliction of shame and disgrace that befall people with mental illnesses. We have pushed legislation for health insurance to have better mental health coverage. We have developed better support systems. The media has done an excellent job with getting the word out to the public that mental illness is a true and treatable medical condition. We still have a long way to go before mental illness can be viewed on the same plane as a physical illness, but we are headed in the right direction.

With the high prevalence of mental illnesses in our society, chances are that you know someone, or are afflicted yourself, with a mental illness. I believe that we are all connected in this world, like the ripple effect of a wave; thus, it behooves us to help another fellow human.

This chapter is not intended to diagnose or treat the reader. Rather, the purpose is to bring awareness to mental health illnesses (which are treatable), as well as letting the audience know that suffering or suicide is not the answer.

If you feel like you are suffering with a mental illness, please seek treatment. You can start with your primary care physician, primary care provider, or counselor. Suicide crisis lines and support groups are available. You do not have to suffer in silence. You are not less of a person. You are not weak. Treatment is available. Just as the clouds part and the sun shines on this Earth, your black cloud can also be lifted to show bright days ahead.

TEACHERS — OUR GREATEST ASSET

When I was in medical school and residency, the saying "See one, do one, teach one" was a standard process for learning. "Seeing one" meant that our mentor showed us how to perform a clinical skill, such as drawing blood or putting in a central line. "Doing one" allowed us to have hands-on learning with the supervision of our mentor. "Teaching one" forced us to demonstrate that we were adept at the taught skill and thereby able to pass our knowledge along to others.

Knowledge is power, and we can obtain knowledge through the learning process. By reading, listening, and viewing new information, we increase our knowledge base. When we are taught how to assimilate this knowledge, we convert the power into usable energy. Teachers are our vessels in guiding us toward this usable knowledge.

Everyone—I repeat, *everyone*—has received direction and been influenced by a teacher. Even self-taught individuals had teachers develop the preparation needed for their success. Brilliant minds, inventors, and entrepreneurs were provided a basic foundation from educators, allowing them to create and advance their craft.

When we were infants, our parents or others were there teaching us how to walk, talk, eat, and play. We were guided through our childhood years by instructors who committed their time to us. Our minds were molded further through high school and college, again by the aid of educators.

Primary and secondary education teachers dedicate their careers to advancing the minds of children and adolescents. The great majority of them spend four years in college to receive a bachelor's degree and they even go on to get an educational certification. Some teachers pursue advanced preparation with master's or doctoral degrees.

These men and women have a passion for teaching. Unfortunately, all too often, the financial burden of their education outbalances their yearly salary. These individuals will almost reach retirement age before their college debt is paid off. In a society where professional athletes get paid millions of dollars per year, we need to rethink the salaries of our dedicated teaching force.

The typical day of a teacher consists of more than arriving at the classroom by 8 a.m. and heading home at 3 p.m. Those are only the school day hours. Teachers continually have to prepare for the days and weeks ahead. This preparation can take them several hours each night. They are also responsible for grading tests and reports that add additional time to their already busy day. Often, in order to get proper sleep on a school night, they spend their weekends staying abreast of their teaching duties.

You might be thinking, "Yeah, that's tough and all, but they get summers, semester breaks, and holidays off." Teachers often start their work duties one to two weeks before school starts, which puts most of them at the end of July or the beginning of August. They finish the school year about a week after the students do. That leaves them with about eight weeks of summer time. After spending fifty to sixty hours per week during the school year, and being on salary with no overtime pay, our educators are putting more time into their duties than most people realize.

But our dedicated teachers don't usually stop there with their school duties. They pick an extracurricular school activity and help lead or support these important endeavors. They may or may not get paid a pittance of a stipend for this work. Yet, they still choose to add additional hours to their already-busy workload.

We demand that our teachers exemplify a code of ethics that we do not expect or request from other professions. Teachers must demonstrate integrity, honesty, and responsibility, both in and out of the classroom. They need to instill hope and trust in their students. Developing mutual respect for one another is imperative if teachers are to reach all of the students. Teachers need to stay informed themselves, keeping up to date on the best teaching methods and styles. Educators must show empathy, fairness, and compassion to each child. They need to be able to pull out the best from their students, while getting them to stay curious and eager about learning. Successful teachers must not only be willing to teach but be amenable to learning from their students.

Elementary and secondary education teachers are not only required to teach their subject to students, but they have to teach life lessons to children and adolescents. As many parents can attest, after being forced to be both parents and teachers during the coronavirus pandemic, this is a very difficult, stressful, and energy-sucking task. Yet, teachers do this without question and without pay. These dedicated individuals know what the stakes are and the disasters that can occur if they don't commit fully to their students. Watching their students succeed in life is rewarding and fulfilling, even if it doesn't pay the pills.

My wife, Angie, epitomizes what a person needs to do in order to be a competent, dedicated, and loving teacher. She has spent her career educating middle schoolers not only about the subject at hand but about life in general. Angie is largely responsible for creating a strong educational foundation for our daughter, Ling, who is now thriving in high school. Our society owes a lot more to teachers like my wife than we have chosen to give.

Men and women who commit their lives to advancing the lives of our children are invaluable. Not only are these people heroes to us, but they pour the foundation by which we reach our heights. Yes, teachers are indeed our greatest asset.

BE YOURSELF: YOUR GREATEST GIFT TO THE WORLD

Imagine a world where all human beings looked, talked, dressed, and acted alike. The monotony of human existence would be disturbingly eerie. Originality and creativity would not exist. Personality would not even be a word in the dictionary, and facial expressions would dissipate. The joy of living would be sucked away, and we would all fall into a robotic state.

Fortunately, this climate does not exist for us. We each have a unique genetic makeup and different life experiences that help define who we are. The diversity of our various personalities, languages, and cultures make for an interesting and enriching environment. We are unique in our own way, and we should stay that way.

When we are born, our bodies are created from the genetic fusion of a female egg and male sperm. From this genetic code, along with what happens to us in utero, we are born with uniquely identifying features. Our fingertips will have marks that only can be traced back to us. We will have a specific hair color, eye color, and facial features. Even identical twins will have body markings that are different from their twin.

As we grow, we will develop languages and accents that are reflective of our environment. We will learn rituals and customs that are specific to our family's way of life. Our personality will start to show through as early as our infancy, and it will continue to progress as we age. We will have characteristics of being extroverted or introverted, insightful or confused, carefree or driven, emotional or stoic, or a wide spectrum along the continuum with a combination of various other characteristics. Our personality will be like that. Like our fingerprint, it is unique to each of us.

Along the way, we will develop features about ourselves that we absolutely love and others that we loathe. Other people may notice and point out our good and bad traits. These traits may be nurtured or corralled by our view of ourselves or the view others have toward us. In order to stay balanced and happy, it is imperative that we protect our positive traits and work to extinguish our negative ones.

For the majority of us, we are able to distinguish between our positive and negative traits. Some of us are unable to untangle the traits and need assistance from others. Furthermore, a small portion of the population is unable to discern these traits to the point that they become pathologic, thereby needing professional guidance.

Of course, all of this is not black and white. A specific trait may be conceived as positive in one person and negative in another. As we are complex beings, so are our personalities and traits that lead us to do what we do and live how we live. The ethical code that we use to guide our lives further influences these outcomes.

That being said, our uniqueness is the greatest gift that we give to the world. One person may discover that they excel in the sciences, whereas others find excitement in law or the arts. By building on these foundations, these individuals may go on to find a cure for cancer, advance civil rights, or touch others in song. It is important, however, that we are in sync with our career choice. The underlying happiness we feel in our lives will have a direct effect and impact on our career outcomes and vice-versa.

The main gift that we give to the world is not just based on our career choice but on the actual uniqueness of our being. The way someone smiles, talks and walks, as well as their mannerisms and behaviors, touch other people. We are all connected in this world. When I was younger, I despised my height and my voice. I wanted my calves to be larger and my buttocks to be smaller. While I am continuing to improve my physical well-being, I have come to love the way I look and the way I talk. There is no one exactly like me, just as there is no one exactly like you.

So then what about cosmetic measures that are utilized to transform the appearance of a person? When I was a teenager, I had a large benign mole on the right side of my chin. I didn't like the mole, and since it was raised, it would bleed whenever I would shave. My parents allowed me to get it removed by a cosmetic surgeon through elective surgery. We justified the surgery due to the shaving irritation, but I quietly loved the way I looked without the mole. Did I fundamentally change my essence? Some will say that I did because I should have not altered my God-given body. However, it was certainly justified due to the potential medical complications of a persistently irritated skin lesion. Surgeons routinely perform many other cosmetically altering surgeries that are medically justified and necessary, such as repairs to cleft lips and cleft palates or nasal and chin surgeries, to name the more common ones. Surgeries such as breast augmentation after breast cancer resections or facial reconstruction after traumas also are medically justified.

But what about surgeries that are purely cosmetic, such as chemical peels, breast implants, or face-lifts? Because of our uniqueness, we will react differently with our aging process. Some of us may embrace it, while others fight it the entire way. As long as these individuals are competent and do not have a body dysmorphic disorder, who am I to tell them no? People can still be able to have these body-altering surgeries and yet stay true to their unique identity.

Now, there will be times when it becomes necessary to conform in certain situations. Children may be required to wear standard uniforms to school. This does not change who they are, but it will put all the children on the same playing field, regardless of their family's financial situation. It also allows the children to focus on their studies rather than their neighbor's clothing. We are expected to have a certain business attire when we are at work, again to focus on the task at hand. Even in these instances, we are able to allow our individuality to shine through in our voices and actions.

All of this chatter is meant to get the point across that we are all special, unique individuals in this world. Too many times, people spend unnecessary energy either conforming themselves or trying to conform others to a preconceived norm. No one has ever been or ever will be like me or you. By accepting the foundation of our uniqueness, and by nurturing and protecting it, we can make ourselves the great gift to the world. So, embrace who you are, and let your beautiful light shine on this world. Thanks for just being you.

OUR ADOPTION STORY

Like many couples and sometimes individuals, my wife Angie and I always wanted to have a family. The first five years of our marriage, we spent our time together building a strong foundation with the plan to one day start a family. By 2003, as our marital sacramental bond yearned to be fulfilled with a child of our own, we proceeded with our plan to conceive a child.

Our attempts were halted by the eventual realization that we were an infertile couple and biological offspring were not in God's plan for us. This disturbance in our lives brought an angst typical of couples confronted with such an ordeal. We jumped through the various hoops to investigate why we couldn't conceive, and by 2004, we accepted our fate that God's plan differed from our perceived one.

In 2004, we contemplated adoption as a means to fulfill our lives with a child, but we found ourselves with a different adoption process that year. In February 2004, we adopted our pet cat Jake and in November 2004 our pet dog Maggie. These blessings helped lay the groundwork that allowed me and Angie to realize that we were able to have a child in our lives. Couples contemplating having a family are told by people to get a dog first and see how that goes, while others say that a pet is no comparison to having children. In our case, the former suggestion was fitting, as Maggie's addition to our family was the critical link to us accepting the enormous responsibilities that occur with having a child.

Prior to having Maggie in our lives, we led a carefree existence. We would leave for weekend trips on a whim, and other than returning for work, we did not worry about when we needed to arrive home. Though we had cats as pets, if left with enough litter and food, they are pretty self-sufficient; a dog, on the other hand, changes the game. Maggie allowed us to really take the necessary steps to care for another living being. She essentially pulled in our reins and let us see that we at least had the potential and selflessness to accept a child in our lives.

Maggie and Jake fulfilled our lives the year they came to live with us, but by 2005, these fellow creatures were not enough to sustain that fulfillment. God's promise to us was made real for me and my wife for the first time on March 20, 2005. We believe that God promised us a child, and though we never stopped believing in his awesome power, we honestly had our doubts about what really was promised to us.

Though there has been no medical proof that a female can determine the exact moment that her child was conceived, many women will attest to having this experience. Yet with adoptive families, we are blessed in that our conception period is the day we start the process of adopting a child. Our conception day was on Sunday, March 20, 2005.

We were visiting my parents in St. Louis for an extended weekend. That Sunday, we went to mass at my childhood parish, St. Gabriel the Archangel Catholic Church. During the celebration, Angie and I both noticed a Caucasian couple with an Asian baby. We assumed that the infant had been adopted by them. Looking at each other, we simultaneously had "conceived" Rebecca Ling at that moment in time. We had been checking out adoption agencies previously, and we were leaning toward Children's Hope International (CHI) agency. It just so happened that CHI had an informational meeting that afternoon. On our trips to St. Louis, we typically left after mass to return to our home in Springfield, Missouri, but that weekend we were staying over until Monday. We felt all these factors to be signs from God that a child was to be ours, just as He had promised to Abraham and Sarah.

After mass, Angie and I were on a high and we couldn't wait until the afternoon CHI meeting; we spent the time putting the cart before the horse as we went to Target looking at baby clothes and toys. Finally, the meeting had arrived, and we listened to two families who had adopted children from Russia and China. We learned about their trials and tribulations and heard how these families muscled through the adoptive process. We spent over an hour afterward talking with these families and CHI personnel; we were so excited and pumped about getting one step closer to Rebecca Ling. We left with a positive and uplifting spirit in our hearts. We spent the rest of the evening chatting with my parents about our plans. We immediately started the process to adopt our little girl from China.

Our "pregnancy" did not last the typical nine months; it was over twenty-two months in length. The gestation period was filled with a roller coaster of emotions. Exhilaration would be followed by disappointment, then excitement, fear, concern, hope, and joy. The year 2006 was coming to a close, and we had heard rumors that China would be further delaying the adoption process.

On Thursday, November 30, 2006, our lives changed forever. Below is the entry that I wrote in the journal I was keeping for my daughter:

> *WONDERFUL NEWS TODAY! We received our first news about you today from Meg at CHI. Your name is Feng Chao Ling, and you were born on 12/4/05. You are presently living in the Anhui Province at the Chaohu Juchao District Children's Welfare Institute. You received a good health report on 9/28/06 with a height of 68 cm (26.8 in), weight of 7kg (15.4 lbs) and normal labs including Hepatitis B immunity. You have 4 teeth (two upper maxillary and two lower mandibular). Your first name Chao means nest and your middle name Ling means clever and nimble and tinkling of precious jade. We are told you are beautiful and tomorrow your mother and I will get our first glimpse of you. Your Godmother informed me that your birthday is the Feast of St. John of Damascus.*

The next day, as fate would have it, we received eleven inches of snowfall and a half an inch of ice, causing our employers to close their doors for the day. We were receiving our informational packet about our daughter. When the UPS driver brought us the paperwork, he allowed me to take his picture. He was our baby-delivering stork, after all. Together, my wife and I received the first glimpse of our daughter in a single photograph, and she was beautiful. I will tell you that I have tears in my eyes as I write these words, living that momentous moment all over again. Interestingly and most notably, from the time we decided to adopt our daughter until her birth, exactly thirty-seven weeks had passed, the typical gestation period for a human being.

Finally, on Monday, January 22, 2007, this wondrous child of God was placed in our arms, and the next day, we officially committed to the Chinese government that she would be ours forever. God's promise to us had been fulfilled and we were with child. I will tell you that the love my wife and I have for this child is as unconditional and real as biological parents have for their children.

These days, Rebecca Ling Pace, who goes by Ling, is a gorgeous, well-adjusted, responsible, and intelligent teenager. She has a love for animals, music, and art, and a yearning to excel in all her affairs. We are a happy family and look forward to the years ahead. If you are contemplating having a child, and have a strong foundation, I strongly encourage you to welcome children into your lives. As I can attest, it doesn't matter if they are generated from your own physical makeup or someone else's genetic code. You will discover that they are your child, through and through.

PROTECTING THE ENVIRONMENT

Imagine walking around your home and stepping into garbage—squishing your feet into rotten banana peels, slipping on plastic soda rings, or wondering what that god-awful smell is emanating from your refrigerator. We certainly wouldn't want our household to be a garbage can of filth. Yet a lot of us treat the environment as if it were our trashcan.

No matter your position on global warming, we can all agree that protecting our environment is the right thing to do. In surveys, the majority of respondents have consistently expressed a desire to protect our world; yet, there is still a significant percentage who has no desire to do so. Perhaps it is because these people do not realize how easy it is to keep our planet clean, or maybe they just don't know how to protect it from themselves. Others don't feel it is necessary and, even more sadly, are the ones who simply don't care. Let's explore some simple ways that we can effortlessly protect our environment and then progress to some more elaborate methods.

The simplest and one of the most effective measures that we can start with today is to simply reduce our waste and consumption of goods. We have become a gluttonous society. With the simple task of pushing away our bodies from the dining room table and putting down our forks when we are satiated, we will reduce natural human waste, consume fewer goods, and in the process, become healthier ourselves. Reducing our meat consumption and conserving our water are easy and significant measures that will keep our planet healthy.

Unfortunately, we have become a throwaway society. We are becoming dependent on and are demanding instant gratification to satisfy our desires. We have confused differences between our needs and or desires. We resort to drinking water from plastic containers, purchasing one-meal microwave dishes with throwaway containers, and allowing companies to sell us goods with non-recyclable products or unnecessary, elaborate packaging. These products end up in landfills and in the oceans, places that are already clogged up with our waste. By principally changing this mindset, even with baby steps, our efforts will go a long way toward protecting our planet. Simple tasks, such as purchasing reusable products and filling up our water bottles from the tap or filtered tap, will be a tremendous benefit to the Earth. We can progress further by recycling our waste, purchasing sustainable goods from eco-friendly companies, and demanding that others help reduce unnecessary waste.

We often hear of reducing our carbon footprint, but we may not know what that means. The amounts of carbon dioxide and methane we emit have direct effects on the potential for global warming. Our carbon footprint is the level of these greenhouse gases we have produced individually or as a group. The significance of this effect is a matter for debate, but most scientists agree that it is a debilitating and significant factor in global warming. Personally, I used to believe that global warming was a hoax, but by educating myself and reviewing the scientific data, I am now a believer. I was angered by politicians and celebrities who told me I needed to walk to work or turn out my lights at night, while they were flying around in private jets and living in extravagant mansions. But again, no matter what your stance is on global warming, we can all agree that pollution is never really a good thing. Pollution may be a result of good things happening in our world, but in itself, it is a terrible byproduct.

In any case, we can alter our carbon footprint in positive ways by utilizing public transportation when possible, walking or riding a bicycle to work or for short trips, and even carpooling. Hopefully in time, electric-powered vehicles will not only replace gas-powered vehicles but become more affordable to the public. The pollution produced by auto emissions is staggering. We must be somewhat patient, though, as switching to all electric or alternative-powered vehicles will take time. We must realize that time will, however, eventually run out, and then it will be too late.

We can ramp up our efforts in saving our planet in more elaborate ways. We can install solar panels in our homes, plant trees, and make compost. Solar power provides clean, renewable energy, and it also decreases our reliance on fossil fuels. More trees on Earth result in decreased levels of atmospheric carbon dioxide and an increased production of oxygen for our environment. Composting reduces landfill waste, reduces use of dangerous pesticides and fertilizers, and recycles our biodegradable trash.

We can all become educators and supporters of a healthy environment. This can involve reminding our friend to put their trash in the recycling bin or telling a family member to turn off the faucet while they are brushing their teeth. We can continue to read about ways to help our environment. We can volunteer with outreach programs and organizations and share our knowledge with others. We may even choose to make a career out of saving the environment while at the same time taking the necessary steps in our own lives in order to protect Mother Earth.

The bottom line is that environmental protection is a responsibility that we all share as human beings. Protecting the Earth is necessary, and we are all capable of helping out. Take baby steps if that is what it will take to start. We all need to take the obligatory steps toward saving our planet.

A Museum Is Just Waiting for You

The purpose of a museum is to procure, display, study, and protect objects that have lasting value or interest. Like a lot of people, I absolutely love visiting museums, especially when I am on vacation. Others despise these places. Yet I hope to convince those despisers that a museum exists out there for everyone's taste.

Art lovers, the paintings are on the wall. This type of museum is probably the first thing that comes to mind when people think of museums. Art museum collections consist of items that visually communicate to the viewer, and these can include paintings, decorative artwork, sculptures, and other works of art. These museums also host other artistic venues in the performing arts arena. Art museums not only convey current works of art but also historical and significant pieces. When I was growing up, I loved going to the St. Louis Art Museum as this majestic building sat atop Art Hill in Forest Park. Visiting the museum was like going to the library with its reverent atmosphere and quiet surroundings. I have also been fortunate enough to visit the Metropolitan Museum of Art in New York City.

History buffs, let's turn back time. This is probably the broadest and most encompassing category of museums. Almost every other museum type could fit under this title. History museums, as the name implies, are collections of significant historical works of art and science that convey the past to the viewer. These collections may consist of artifacts, clothing, videos, newspaper clippings, reconstructions, and other means of displaying historical times.

The history museum is the one type of museum that seems to be able to touch us all. Though a lot of people may not like the thought of studying history, they can find a history museum that will pique their interest. Visitors can explore museums that offer information about their city, region, or state. War buffs can visit war and presidential museums. Sports buffs can visit various sports museums. Museums exist for car and transportation buffs, animal lovers, and other specific subjects. Specialty museums, such as Graceland in Memphis, Tennessee, and World of Coca-Cola in Atlanta, Georgia, appeal to the masses. The general museum, which can fit into the history category, is a multidisciplinary museum that contains collections of different subjects. Almost anyone can find something interesting for them in these museums. I love visiting the smaller local area museums, as I often discover hidden gems in these places. I was also fortunate to see firsthand the Terracotta Warriors at the museum of the same name in Xi'an, Shaanxi, China.

Science explorers, it is time for blast-off. This is another broad category of museums that can encompass subjects in science, technology, space, and exploration. These museums usually combine historical displays with interactive and instructive activities for the guest. Visitors are able to come out of the museum with experiences that enable them to have a better appreciation and understanding of how science works. I often leave these facilities with a sense of awe. I recall seeing the stars at the St. Louis Planetarium growing up and being excited when they expanded the museum to what it is today. My jaw dropped when I visited the Smithsonian Air and Space Museum in Washington, D.C., and I recalled my childhood dreams of yearning to be an astronaut when I visited NASA's Kennedy Space Center at Cape Canaveral on Merritt Island, Florida.

Outdoorsman and environmentalists, we've got Earth uncovered for you. Natural history and natural science museums consist of collections relating to the natural world. These museums may contain animals, insects, rocks, fossils, plants, and similar specimens of this world. They usually convey and act on the history, conservation, and projected future of our environment. The movie *Night at the Museum* really brought this type of museum into the forefront of viewers' minds. I have been to several of these museums around the country but the Field Museum in Chicago, Illinois, is my favorite.

Children, it is time to come out and play. Children's museums, as the name implies, are places meant to provide learning opportunities for children. They are often filled with exhibits and informal programs that stimulate the child's brain for a unique learning experience. I have never met a child who doesn't want to visit one of these museums. When my daughter was a child, we would often search for a children's museum when traveling out of town. We have been to several of them, and as parents can attest that visiting one of these museums can be as memorable and joyful for the parent as much as the child. My daughter's and my favorite children's museum is in my own hometown of St. Louis, Missouri. The City Museum, however, is much more than a children's museum, as it is a place of wonder for the young and old. Rather than try and describe it, I'll let City Museum do it, since they describe it the best:

About City Museum: "Housed in the ten-story, 600,000 square-foot warehouse of the International Shoe Company, City Museum is a mixture of children's playground, funhouse, surrealistic pavilion, and architectural marvel made out of found and repurposed objects. The brainchild of internationally acclaimed artist Bob Cassilly, a classically trained sculptor, City Museum opened for visitors in 1997."

Aquatic aficionados, let's make a splash. Whether or not aquariums can be classified as museums doesn't really matter because I am adding them to this list. Aquariums are institutions that house and display fish and other aquatic life for the visitor. They often are linked to conservation efforts with teams working to protect these fellow creatures. I always feel more connected with Mother Earth when I see a dolphin, sea otter, or penguin up close. Aquariums can be found in zoos, museums, and as standalone facilities. My favorite and most memorable visit to an aquarium was seeing Winter live during filming of the movie *Dolphin Tale*. Winter lives at the Clearwater Marine Aquarium in Clearwater, Florida. Coincidentally, a follow-up visit found us being able to meet and listen to a question-and-answer session from the director and actors of the movie *Dolphin Tale 2*.

Candle makers, don't light one in this museum. Wax museums are scattered throughout our land with impressive and realistic wax sculptures. They usually contain sculptures of historical and contemporary famous people. I can tell you that these figures almost appear alive, as I have been able to visit probably the most famous and recognizable wax museum, Madame Tussauds.

Computer geeks, peer into your screen for a virtual museum visit. For a number of reasons, we may not be able to physically visit a museum. Fortunately, many museums now have websites that allow for virtual visits. So, crank up your computer or head to the library for some real-time fun and exploration.

Finally, if you can't muster up excitement for any of the museums listed above, you will likely admire the architectural creations that often house these institutions. Just look at the Guggenheim Art Museums in New York City and Bilbao, Spain. Oh, and yes, there are museums for architecture and design as well.

PATRIOTIC HEROES

What does it mean to be a patriotic hero? Patriotism is a devotion or love that one has for his/her country. We all have our own idea of what a hero means to us. Often, when we think of patriotic heroes, the military, police force, and fire and rescue groups come to mind.

I have always had a fondness for the military. Though I never served in the military, I see the reasons why countries maintain a means to protect themselves. I used to believe that we didn't really owe much to the enlisted men and women that have served in the military. Sure, I thought that we were forever indebted to those individuals who were drafted against their will, but the people enlisting chose to join the military.

It turns out I was very ignorant in my view on the enlisted military personnel. It really doesn't matter what their intentions were for joining the military. When I started treating military veterans, I learned the true sacrifices that these men and women made in serving our country and protecting our citizens.

We all know that the military sends their troops off to battle and conflicts, but no one is ever prepared for the casualties of war. Our young men and women who have served or fought in wars come back with physical and psychological scars. They may have to live the rest of their lives walking around without limbs, endure realistic and horrifying flashbacks, or have their sleep disturbed by frightful nightmares. Some give the ultimate sacrifice and make it home in a body bag.

Imagine being a 130-pound soldier toting around your weight in gear and armor as you walk around scouting the area. After months and years of this routine, wear-and-tear injuries can occur that cause chronic and sometimes debilitating pain.

When you apply for a job in the private sector, you are given a duty description knowing your expectations with the position. However, that's not the case when you join the military. Though you may have anticipated a certain job title, you may be required to do a completely different job. Physical or psychological ailments may haunt military veterans due to being thrust into duties that they were either not physically equipped or mentally prepared to perform.

Our military veterans deserve the respect, admiration, and any compensation that we can provide them. Whether you are a supporter or opponent of the military, you should be able to see the patriotic heroism that is characteristic of our military personnel and veterans.

Another period that was so evident of patriotic heroism was in the aftermath of 9/11. Most adults can recall exactly what they were doing on the day of September 11, 2001, when our country was under attack by terrorists. On that somber day in our American history, men and women in uniform selflessly ran into harm's way.

Police, firefighters, and rescue personnel put their own well-being aside and acted quickly and purposefully to assist their fallen brothers and sisters. Though they may have been confused and uncertain about the situation at hand, these professional first responders responded with heroic and lifesaving measures. Some of them lost their lives that day, while others died in the following weeks, months, and years.

Today, our first responders are still carrying out patriotic heroic acts by just showing up for work. They don't know what each day brings, what hazards they will face, or what obstacles they will need to overcome. Yet they still show up for their shift, hoping and eager to make someone's unfortunate situation better with their skill, empathy, and knowledge.

For comic book aficionados, patriotic superheroes like Superman, Captain Marvel, and Wonder Woman come to mind. Though our patriotic human heroes cannot techni-cally perform superhuman feats, they do indeed carry out mind-boggling acts daily. Whereas most of us would be running out of a burning house, firefighters are deliber-ately heading toward the flames.

More recently, with the coronavirus pandemic, our health professionals have been in the limelight. By being essential workers and carrying out our duties, we have been viewed as among the everyday heroes. What's interesting about all the heroes described is that they have a common thread; they say they don't feel like heroes because they are just doing their jobs.

I would be remiss if I didn't mention teachers in this mix of patriotic heroes. Teachers collectively work to see that their pupils advance in their education. Educators tirelessly work for the good of our society. They are heroes in my book.

Indeed, countless other heroes could be named. My understanding of a patriotic hero is anyone who works to make sure that the values and ideals of their country are brought to life and are being upheld. The United States has made some mistakes along the way, but our Constitution is worth fighting for and protecting.

We must be cognizant and be able to decipher the true meaning of patriotism. Patriotism means a love for one's country and believing in the basic laws and constitutions of that country. It does not mean a love for leadership. Hopefully, our leadership will be true and loyal patriots. When our leaders deviate from our Constitution, we must be wary of their position and be able to stand strong for our country's foundation.

Many patriots believe that their country is the greatest country on Earth. The United States is one of those countries where many citizens and immigrants take that position. I am proud to be an American. I hope one day that all Americans will be able to feel that way as well. In order to reach that goal, we will need to fight for our Constitution and our way of life for all of our inhabitants.

GET MOVING

The human body was meant and designed to move and be active. Our prehistoric ancestors relied on their bodies in order to scavenge for food, escape from danger, and protect themselves. As our being evolved, we discovered ways to make our lives more comfortable. In the process, we essentially eliminated the survival factor.

Though we still have the instinctual drive to survive, the various factors for our survival are, in essence, done for us. Our food is gathered for us, we have uniformed forces for protection, and our transportation no longer relies on our own two feet. In the process, we have allowed our bodies to become sedentary.

According to the National Center for Health Statistics, just over half of the adults in the United States, 18 years of age and older, have met the minimum physical activity standards for aerobic activity. That number plummets to less than a quarter of the population when both aerobic and muscle-strengthening activity standards were factored together.

The current minimum recommendation for children and adolescents is one hour of vigorous activities per day. Adults 18 years of age and older should get one hundred and fifty minutes of moderately vigorous activity or seventy-five minutes of vigorous activity per week. Muscle-strengthening activity recommendations are three and two times per week for adolescents and adults respectively.

So why don't we exercise? Many factors are involved, but the main reason as a culture is that we have substituted body inactivity for body movement. We drive our cars or take the bus to work rather than walk or ride our bikes. We select our foods from a sign at a drive-thru food establishment or sit down at a restaurant to an oversized meal portion. This replaces our previous need to tend to the crops and butcher the meats. We sit down watching television or playing video games in the evenings rather than going outside to play.

We have convinced our minds that the above scenarios are luxuries and a progressive evolution of humans. In some instances, they are beyond our control. Often we cannot afford or are not willing to live near our work, so it becomes essential that we substitute our transportation needs from self to motor-assisted mobility. In other instances, we spend our time focused on our career choice and leave the food industry to others as their chosen careers.

Yet none of this negates the fact that our bodies were meant to move. We all realize this need. Just look at all of the fitness clubs, exercise programs, and sporting activities that are available. Almost a quarter of our population accepts and actively sets their bodies in motion in order to reach their minimum activity standards. The rest of us either meet some of the standards or choose not to be active at all.

When the word exercise is mentioned, most people have excuses as to why they don't exercise. But I never really hear anyone give an excuse as to why they don't watch television. If they were unable to watch their favorite shows for some reason, they probably had them taped for another slothful night. You may be thinking, "Whoa! I'm not a sloth," and though that may be true, being slothful is simply being indolent or having an aversion to movement.

We need to rethink our need and desire for exercise. Exercise for a lot of people is a bad word. We have many excuses for why we are unable to exercise, and though some are valid, many are not. When most people think of exercise, they envision themselves laboriously doing a repetitive and boring activity. We need to simply think about moving more for our health and for enjoyment. We are more accepting of being active than exercising, even though they are essentially the same thing.

The great thing about being active is that nearly everyone can do it immediately and have fun while doing it. This could be a simple activity such as walking with your dog or with a friend. We may choose to go bike riding, play tennis, golf without a cart, swim, or select from an almost endless list of fun activities. The key is finding an activity that is fun, rewarding, and lasting. Some people choose to participate in multiple activities for diversity or various other reasons.

I often hear from patients that they are too out of shape or have chronic debilitating illnesses that prevent them from being active. Very few people are unable to be more active. We have evidence-based outcome studies that rhythmic activities such as tai chi and yoga help improve chronic pain, increase flexibility, and improve one's overall health. We have shown that water activities such as swimming and water aerobics have lower impact on the body. Even chair aerobics allows the most inactive person to get moving.

The benefits of becoming and staying active with the minimum standards are vast. An active person may be happier, lose or maintain weight more easily, improve sleep, reduce pain, and decrease their risk for developing chronic diseases more than an inactive person.

Human beings were meant to have active bodies. It may be difficult initially to get the ball rolling. However, once set in motion, inertia takes over, and the next thing you know, our sedentary bodies become forces of active energy. So, let's get moving, and just maybe I'll see you out on the trails.

REFERENCES/ WEBSITES OF INTEREST

Why Everyone Should Visit My Hometown
References & Websites Of Interest

https://www.stlouis-mo.gov/visit-play/stlouis-history.cfm

https://www.gatewayarch.com

https://www.mlb.com/cardinals/

https://www.nhl.com/blues

https://www.stlambush.com

https://www.stlcitysc.com

https://www.forestparkforever.org/visit

https://www.stlouisunionstation.com

http://www.stlthepolarexpressride.com

https://www.citymuseum.org

http://citygardenstl.org

https://www.grantsfarm.com

https://www.magichouse.org

https://www.sixflags.com/stlouis

https://www.anheuser-busch.com/
about/breweries-and-tours.html

https://www.missouribotanicalgarden.org/
media/fact-pages/butterfly-house.aspx

https://www.missouribotanicalgarden.org

https://www.fabulousfox.com

https://jazzstl.org

https://www.slso.org

http://www.thechaifetzarena.com

http://www.stifeltheatre.com

https://www.thegrandel.com

https://www.thesheldon.org

https://www.cunetto.com

https://www.mcgurks.com

http://www.360-stl.com

https://www.stlballparkvillage.com

https://www.tonysstlouis.com

https://olympiakebobandtavern.com/

https://www.sonesta.com/us/missouri/st-louis/
chase-park-plaza-royal-sonesta-st-louis

https://moonrisehotel.com

https://curiocollection3.hilton.com/en/hotels/
missouri/st-louis-union-station-hotel-curio-col-
lection-by-hilton-STLCUQQ/index.html

https://www.premiumoutlets.com/outlet/st-louis

https://www.mallscenters.com/outlets/
missouri/taubman-prestige-outlets

https://www.visitmarylandheights.org

https://visittheloop.com

https://www.stlouis-mo.gov/live-work/community/
neighborhoods/the-ville/the-ville-overview.cfm

https://explorenorthstlouiscounty.com

http://www.lacledeslanding.com

https://lafayettesquare.org

http://www.soulard.org

https://cwescene.com/

http://www.grandcenter.org

https://www.cherokeeantiquerow.com

http://www.cityofmaplewood.com

http://thegrovestl.com

http://southgrand.org

Bullying
References & Websites Of Interest

https://childrensnational.org/departments/
bullying-related-health-risks

www.aacap.org/AACAP/Families_and_Youth/
Facts_for_Families/FFF-Guide/Bullying-080.aspx

https://www.stopbullying.gov

http://www.apa.org/topics/bullying/

https://medlineplus.gov/bullying.html

https://blogs.scientificamerican.com/
guest-blog/the-origins-of-bullying/

Resolutions
References Websites Of Interest

http://www.history.com/news/
the-history-of-new-years-resolutions

https://www.britannica.com/topic/Janus-Roman-god

https://www.statisticbrain.com/
new-years-resolution-statistics/

http://sphweb.bumc.bu.edu/otlt/MPH-
Modules/SB/BehavioralChangeTheories/
BehavioralChangeTheories6.html

Doran, G. T. (1981). There's a S.M.A.R.T. Way
to Write Management's Goals and Objectives.
Management Review, 70, 35-36.

prd-medweb-cdn.s3.amazonaws.com/documents/
vmcpathology/files/Smart_goals_template.pdf

https://www.webmd.com/fitness-exercise/
guide/smart-weight-loss-fitness-device

O Canada!
References & Websites of Interest

http://aubergesaint-gabriel.com/en/

https://www.basiliquenotredame.ca/en/

http://www.vieux.montreal.qc.ca/eng/accueila.htm

https://www.chateauramezay.qc.ca/en/

https://www.oldportofmontreal.com

http://www.stm.info/en/info/networks/metro

https://www.grayline.com/tours/montreal/montreal-
48-hour-hop-on-hop-off-tour-5867_2_12130_409/

https://www.saint-joseph.org/en/

http://www.go-montreal.com/areas_chinatown.htm

https://www.montrealsciencecentre.com

https://www.lemontroyal.qc.ca/en/

https://www.mcgill.ca

https://montrealundergroundcity.com

https://espacepourlavie.ca/en

https://parcolympique.qc.ca/en/

https://www.quebec-cite.com/en

http://www.lesplainesdabraham.ca/en/

https://www.fairmont.com/frontenac-quebec/

https://www.quebec-cite.com/en/businesses/
funiculaire-du-vieux-quebec

https://www.sepaq.com/destinations/parc-chute-mont-
morency/index.dot?language_id=1

https://www.notre-dame-de-quebec.org/home

A Cuban Adventure
References & Websites Of Interest

https://www.royalcaribbean.com

https://www.conchtourtrain.com

https://hemingwayhome.com

https://www.keylimeshop.com

https://www.keywestaquarium.com

https://www.hotelnacionaldecuba.com

https://whc.unesco.org/en/list/204

http://www.lahabana.com/guide/capitolio/

http://www.lahabana.com/guide/la-bodeguita-del-medio/

http://www.lahabana.com/content/
fuster-cubas-irrepressible-gaudi-restyles-jaimanitas/

http://www.lahabana.com/guide/
castillo-de-los-tres-reyes-del-morro/

http://www.lahabana.com/guide/cristo-de-la-habana/

http://www.porteverglades.net

https://www.flamingogardens.org

https://newrivergroves.com

https://seawatchontheocean.com

Medical Novel Reviews
References

House Calls and Hitching Posts
Dorcas Sharp Hoover www.goodbooks.com

When All The World Was Young
Ferrol Sams www.penguin.com

Aesculapius was a Mizzou Tiger:
an Illustrated History of Medicine at Ol' Mizzou
Hugh E Stephenson Jr., M.D. University of
Missouri Medical School Foundation, Inc.

On Doctoring Stories, Poems, Essays
Edited by Richard Reynolds, M.D. & John
Stone, M.D. Simon and Schuster

The House of God
Sam Shem, M.D. Dell Publishing